INDIANS

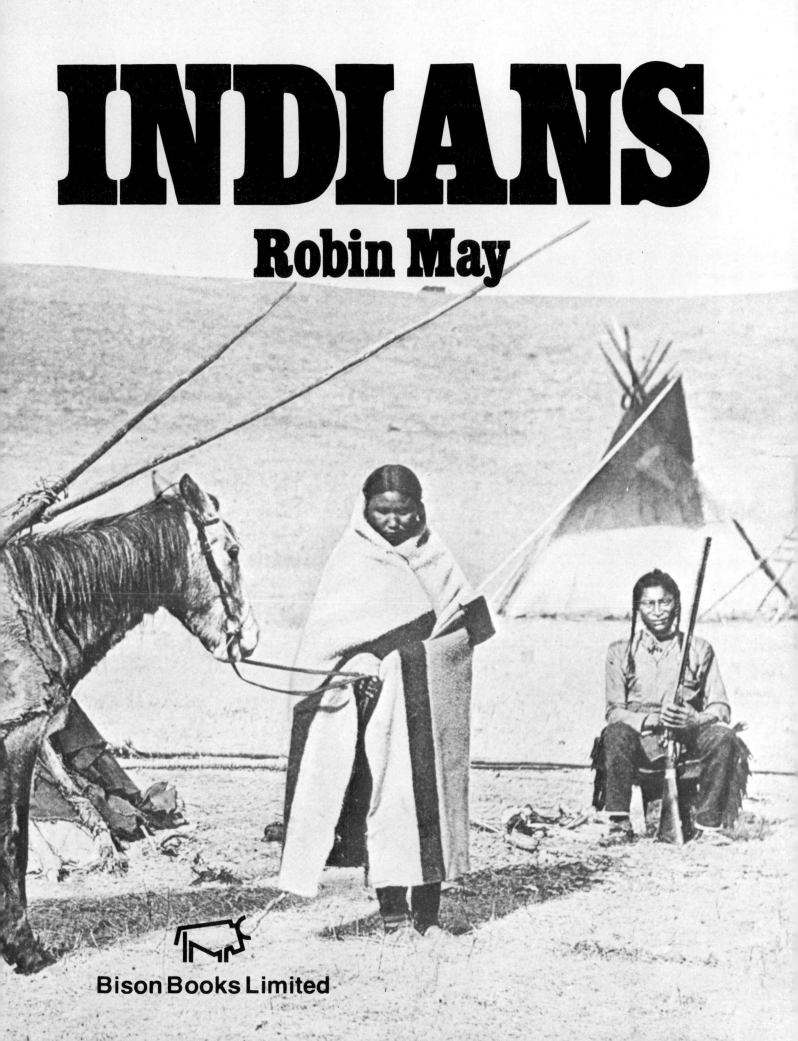

INDIANS
Robin May

Bison Books Limited

Published 1982 by
Bison Books Limited
39 Sloane Street, London SW1

Copyright © 1982 Bison Books Limited

ISBN 0 86124 045 6

Printed in Hong Kong

For
ALLAN
and
MARION RADBOURNE

Half title page: A Hidatsa warrior in the costume of the Dog Dance.

Title page: Horse travois of the Plains Indians.

This page: The Snowshoe Dance of the Chippewa.

CONTENTS

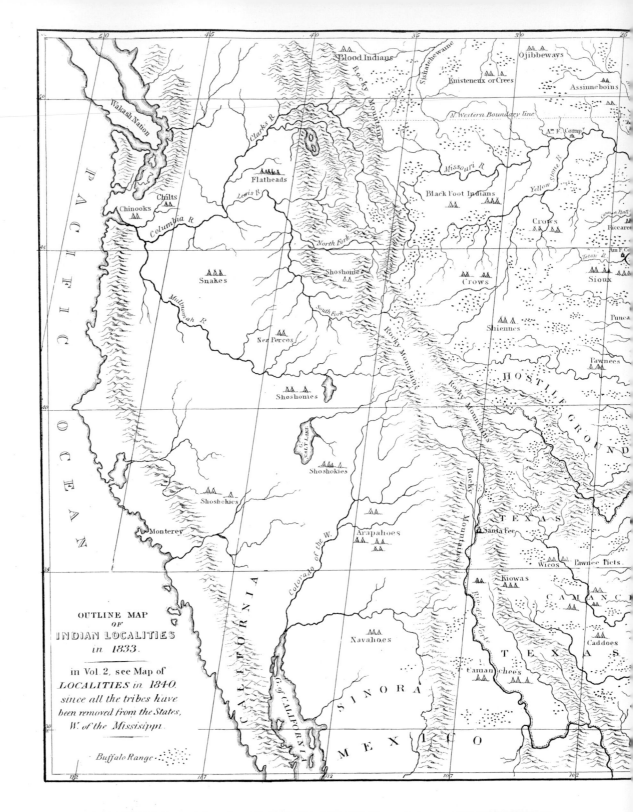

OUTLINE MAP
OF
INDIAN LOCALITIES
in 1833.

in Vol. 2, see Map of
LOCALITIES in 1840,
since all the tribes have
been removed from the States,
W. of the Missisippi.

Buffalo Range

INTRODUCTION AND ACKNOWLEDGMENTS

This book concentrates almost entirely on the Native Americans of what is now the United States. Space permits only a handful of tribes to be described in any detail, otherwise any narrative flow would be impossible. Other tribes are featured at key moments in their history, while many more can be tracked down elsewhere by the interested reader—tribes such as the Winnebago, the Assiniboin, the Kickapoo and dozens more which held the stage for moments of brief fame and less brief tragedy.

Most of this book is about the trans-Mississippi West from the 1850s to 1890, the year of Wounded Knee, though there is a chapter about the Indians of the East who had faced much earlier, in the Colonial period, most of the same

problems with the whites as did the tribes in the West.

The spelling of Indian names and words follows Webster's *Third New International Dictionary*.

The state historical societies of Arizona, South Dakota, Montana, Wyoming and Kansas are among the organizations to which I am grateful. It is in highly researched articles in their journals that previously accepted facts are so often revealed to be untrue. I am particularly grateful to Allan Radbourne for helping me with the complexities of the Apache Wars, and to Robert A Utley, whose books are exactly what scholarly histories of the Indian Wars ought to be but so rarely are. I also owe a great debt to my wife, Maureen, for her encouragement and help.

Robin May

Many Indian tribes worshipped natural phenomena, as seen in *Invocation to the Sun*, painted by Charles M Russell.

1
NATIVE AMERICANS

It happened just before the final tragedy at Wounded Knee brought the Indian Wars to an end. The date was September 1890; the place, Lame Deer in Montana; the Indians involved, two Northern Cheyennes called Head Chief and John Young Mule. Twenty-five-year-old Head Chief was a troublemaker, partly because he was bitter that he had never had a chance to prove himself as a warrior. He was fond of the daughter of Chief American Horse. Food was short, and when the girl told Head Chief this, he went hunting with an orphan boy, John Young Mule, who was 13 or 14 years old.

They set out after deer, but instead shot a cow that belonged to a settler named Gaffney. They had just finished butchering it when Gaffney's nephew, Hugh Boyle, rode up. Young Mule, who had been to school and understood English, told Head Chief that Boyle had said: 'He called us dogs.'

Head Chief grabbed his rifle, shot Boyle and buried him in a shallow grave. Young Mule later reported that Boyle had actually said: 'I see a hungry dog has snapped up one of our cows.'

Soldiers were soon looking for the missing Boyle, first finding his horse, then bloodstains.

Below: Conquistadores setting war dogs on Indians. Right: An engraving of 1590, *The Arrival of the Englishmen in Virginia* by Theodor de Bry. Far right above: Another de Bry engraving of 16th century Virginia Indians. Below: *Virginia Indians Cooking Fish* by John White (1590).

Pasquenoke.

Trinety harbor

T B

Above: Paintings of Aztec Indians in Mexico, c. 1500. Right: This 16th century painting shows a battle between the Aztecs and Cortez's troops.

Meanwhile, the Cheyenne were expecting the whites to attack their camp. When Head Chief realized this, he told American Horse what had happened and asked him to let the soldiers know that he was the guilty one. He would not be hanged, but would fight them all in the open.

Young Mule came to Head Chief and said

Above: *Interior of the Lodge of a Mandan Chief* by Karl Bodmer, c. 1839. Right, clockwise from upper left: Shahaka, chief of the Mandan tribe as painted by Charles Bird King. Mah-To-Toh-Pa, second chief of the Mandans. A Mandan of the 1840s. Assiniboin, Mandan and Pawnee chiefs.

that he would die with him. 'When you are dead, I will have nothing,' he explained. They spent that last night talking on a hill.

At sunrise, the time had come to die. Below the hill were hundreds of Cheyenne, and also cavalry and infantry facing the braves, ready, if necessary, to put down an uprising.

The two Indians charged down the hill, then wheeled up again. Young Mule's horse was hit on the way up and had to be led to the top; then the young man started down the hill again on foot, shooting, zigzagging, taking cover, and shooting again until he was killed. Head Chief, who had told his friends that he would ride straight through the soldiers, donned his grandfather's war bonnet and charged down the hill at a gallop. Hit time and again by bullets, he was still charging through the dismounted sol-diers when an officer shot him fatally. The sol-

Top row, left to right: A Nootka whaling Indian from the Northwest Coast; an Osage Indian holding a pipe-tomahawk; White Swan, a Crow warrier with a stone club and rawhide shield. Bottom row, left to right: A Wisham man of the Northwest Coast spearing salmon in the Columbia River; A Southern Cheyenne, Wolf Robe (Ho Níhewoomah), in a photo taken in 1909; a Blackfoot, Bird Rattler, in a photograph taken in Browning, Montana in the year 1916.

diers went away, leaving the Cheyenne to tend to their dead.

That small-scale fight combines the fact and the myth of the American Indian. It is a classic reminder that the story of the American West was not romantic but epic. For many, mounted Plains Indians like the Cheyenne typify the Native Americans, yet most of the northern Plains Indians were mounted for little more than a century—a small part of the 30,000 or so years in which there had been Indians in the Americas.

'Indians' is as vague a word as 'Europeans'. Columbus coined the name when he thought he had reached the Indies—India—in 1492. In recent times 'Amerind' has been coined, though the more recent 'Native American' is a happier phrase. For the purpose of this book, however, Indian will be used. As for calling them 'Redmen', some of the first white men to land in the East saw quite light-skinned Indians. When they tanned in the summer, their skins became reddish, then a fine copper color.

Down the centuries, white attitudes toward Indians have tended to follow two courses, the 'painted savage' or the 'noble savage/downtrodden native'. The vast majority of frontier whites believed bitterly in the first portrait, while farther East, which had once been a frontier, there was more sympathy with the unfortunate Indians. Since the 1950s, the shame of present-day Americans has been based more on an awakened conscience than on knowledge of what the West was really like. It has so distorted the picture that many well-meaning readers of propaganda rather than history have turned the American Indian into an idealized being persecuted by wicked whites, as if all Indians were like the noble Chief Joseph of the Nez Percé and all whites like the monstrous Colonel Chivington of Sand Creek. The truth, of course, lies in between. Indians and whites were—people. Which is not to say that the stricken conscience of many white people is not justified. The Native Americans were greatly wronged and many still are.

Today's revised version of the Indians is as simplistic as the 'painted savage' school of thought. The Indians are praised as ecologists, as warriors who preferred peace, as natural democrats, as a superb example of communal people and as people who understood the natural world. Only the first and the last stand up as generalizations. As Frederick William Turner III has put it, having characterized the harshness of Indian life, 'he never lost sight of the fact that all this was distinctively, essentially, radically human, that he was human and thus part of the universal community of the living.' The harshness included the fact that old people were often brutally treated and that women were usually regarded as second-class citizens.

Before noting what many tribes had in common, let us note a few of the extreme contrasts. Some were caused by geography, others were not. Northwestern Indians in coastal regions had as much respect for property and status as whites had. Most Indians, however, did not. The Natchez had a class structure that included a Sun God at the top and a class of 'Stinkards' at the bottom, which startled even the French. The Choctaw and Chickasaw of the Southeast were neighbors, but were enemies until the 19th century, the former being aggressive, the latter being farmers. And though the Mandan and Caddo hunted buffalo on horseback in the 19th century, they remained farmers and lived in settled villages. The rest of the Plains Indians became nomads once they got the horse. In the Southwest, the Apache roamed the deserts and mountains; the Pueblo lived in stone-built apartment blocks.

Indians differed greatly in appearance and color, and spoke hundreds of different languages belonging to some six major language groups.

Despite these differences, however, along with many others, most tribes, from the lordly Iroquois in the forests of the East to primitive tribes in the deserts of the far West, shared some things in common—beliefs that made a clash with the white man certain. It was not just the clash of Stone Age versus Industrial Age, for Indians were quick to use modern weapons and tools. It was a different view of life. Indians believed that the earth was their mother, not something that could be bought and sold and owned. The earth was a divine gift for all to share, animals as well as humans. It could be farmed for survival and hunted over and fought over, but rarely was it owned in sec-

Top left: A mounted Blackfoot Indian from a painting by Karl Bodmer. Top right: A Crow warrier painted by George Catlin. Bottom: A Cheyenne warrior as painted by the renowned western artist, Frederic Remington.

Opposite: Indians and their horses. Top: *Wild Horses of the American Plains,* from a painting by George Catlin. Center: *Indians Catching Wild Horses,* also by Catlin. Bottom: *The Pursuit,* an 1856 engraving by N Currier.

tions like the white man owned land. Indians were close to the living world. All animals were their brothers, even those whom they hunted to survive. Indians were deeply religious and believed in 'Medicine', the spirit that protected them in everyday life and in battle.

Their communal life was indeed democratic, but democracy often led to anarchy. Indian leaders rarely had the power of white generals, and all too often braves spoiled the effect of an attack because they were entitled to do what they wanted. Personal freedom was all-important, and it was on the warpath that a warrior was expected to make his mark.

War became faster and more exciting with the coming of the horse. By the late 18th century all Plains Indians were mounted on the descendants of escaped Spanish horses. Suddenly war was no longer a slogging match on foot but an almost medieval contest. It became finer to *touch* an enemy with a stick than kill him.

As for torture, it was common enough, especially in the East, but it was common, too, in Europe. Many tribes became more brutal because they were brutally treated by others. It should also be noted that many tribes thought well of captives, Indian or white, who could endure torture. The Iroquois and others greatly

Top left: **Wild rice was one of the staple crops of the Indians of Wisconsin, as this etching shows.**
Top right: **The Spanish conquistadores introduced the horse to the Indians.**

Indian costumes of the 18th century. *A*, Mountain Indian near Hudson's Bay; *B*, Cree woman; *C*, Woman of the Wyandotte (Iroquois) tribe; *D*, Indian of the Mohawk tribe.

honored a prisoner who could shout or sing defiance during torture. They sometimes ate dead heroes, hoping to gain their strength.

What Indians considered utterly barbaric was prison. Joseph Brant, the great Mohawk, was appalled on a visit to England to find that mere debtors were imprisoned. He said he would rather endure the worst tortures at the stake than imprisonment. As for scalping, though it seems to have been of Indian origin, it spread westward across the continent because of the Europeans' habit of offering bounties for scalps.

Warfare was only part of the life of even the most warlike tribe. Though an Indian woman's lot was often exhausting—women normally did the farming—children of both sexes had a wonderful time, living almost without discipline. Family life was, and is, often far closer than that of the whites. And for all the racial hatred

that flared on successive frontiers as atrocity on each side was added to atrocity, many whites envied the Indians' free life, especially in early Colonial times. This view is supported by the number of captives, and not just ones taken in infancy, who preferred to stay Indian even when rescuers arrived. The frontiersmen, who so often hated Indians, frequently lived lives not so very different from them. Indeed the true frontiersmen lost almost as much as the Indians when 'civilization' arrived. There was no place for either in a settled West—but at least the whites were not discriminated against.

Before the ancestors of today's Indians discovered the Americas some 30,000 years ago, those continents were empty of human life. Carbon-14 dating techniques have fixed the approximate time of arrival, though some new find may one day wreck current calculations.

Above: Before the Spanish introduced the horse to the Americans, Indians made use of the dog as a beast of burden. This is a dog travois—the only transport early Indians had.

Top left: Indians sometimes fought on horseback— *Fight to the Finish* **by Charles Schreyvogel. Top right:** *The Indian Method of Breaking a Pony,* **a drawing by Frederic Remington.**

The newcomers came across what is now the Bering Strait. Even today it is only five miles wide with islands in between. Then, during an ice age, the waters were lower and, it is thought, the strait may have been a grassy plain.

Across the plain came humans, some no doubt because of wanderlust, others because Siberia was becoming too ice-bound to support life. Whatever the reasons, they came.

North America was experiencing its own ice age, but there was a vast route free of ice east of the Rockies, and geologists have found another route farther west which could have been used ·as the temperature rose and the ice retreated.

Progress southward must have gone on for many centuries, possibly for 25,000 years. Latecomers, when the Bering Strait was formed, could use small boats like those of today's Eskimo to cross the water.

The greatest achievements of the descendants of the invaders were to be in Mexico and Peru. No northern Indians reached the heights of the Inca and Aztec cultures, though some had notable civilizations by the time the Europeans arrived. In fact, North America was far emptier than the rest of the hemisphere when whites first appeared in the West in 1540. Its Indian population is reckoned at between one and two million, whereas Mexico alone may have had up to 15 million people before disease and killings drastically reduced the population.

Before the Spanish arrived, the Southwest had enjoyed the golden age of the Pueblos (Spanish for towns) those bustling villages four or five stories high that were built in caverns in cliffs, on top of mesas or simply on flat ground. The great age of these experiments in communal living was from the 11th to the 13th centuries. There is a dispute as to why that age

The Buffalo Dance of the Mandan Indians. In this painting by the artist, Karl Bodmer, the Indians are wearing skins and masks to work magic on one of their chief sources of food.

Above: Taos Pueblo, New Mexico. Inset left: A battle between the Anasazi. Inset right: A Navajo Indian of Arizona (1910). Left: A Hopi Indian with a stick thrown to kill rabbits.

ended. Perhaps it was a combination of drought and tension in the pueblos; perhaps it was the arrival from the north of the ancestors of the Apache and the Navaho. However, when the Spanish arrived, the area was still full of life.

They came, some of them on horses, seeking the Seven Cities of Gold. (These were the first horses the Indians had ever seen.) To the conquerors of Mexico and Peru all things seemed possible, reports of golden cities included. Instead, Francisco de Coronado and his men found villages of mud and stone that shone in the distance in the sun. Yet this expedition, which was dubbed a failure, penetrated as far as Kansas. The Grand Canyon was seen and so were the great buffalo herds; and the first wars were fought between whites and Indians in what became the United States. The Zuñi

Top right: Flathead Indian mother and child.

Top right: Flathead Indian mother and child.

fought valiantly to defend their pueblos from the invaders with their terrible weapons—firearms and horses.

The Spaniards did not return until 1581. Then, in 1598, colonists arrived, 400 of them, and the white colonization of North America had begun. With the colonists came cattle, whose straying descendants were to be the Texas cowboys' immortal longhorns. More importantly for the Indians, horses came, whose descendants were to transform so dramatically the lives of the Plains Indians. Weapons, too, spread north and, later, spread west from the Atlantic. Firearms were obtained. Diseases were helping to reduce the number of Indians, making the white man's task far easier. Naturally, the Indians improved their weapons. Arrows soon had metal tips and firearms were obtained, but sheer numbers of men would defeat the Indians in the end, numbers that swelled as other nations reached the New World.

Spaniards had landed in the East as early as the 1530s, when several attempts were made to colonize Florida. An expedition led by a vet-

Center right: Village of the Haida people of British Columbia (1890). Below: Pawnee earth lodges on the Platte River (1870).

Above: Pueblo Indians in *The Lookout*, by W R Leigh. Left: Sequoyah, an Indian scholar who developed a Cherokee alphabet in 1821. Painting by Charles Banks Wilson. Opposite page below: Pigeon's Egg, the head of the Assiniboine tribe, painted by George Catlin in 1831. Top left: *Indians Fishing from a Canoe* in *North Carolina* by John White, c. 1585. Top right: A lithograph by Karl Bodmer showing some tepees of the Assiniboin tribe of Indians.

eran of Peru, Hernando de Soto, in 1539, almost reached Oklahoma, but found no riches. Yet between them, Coronado and de Soto had almost spanned what became the United States.

Before noting the other nations so soon to be on the scene, one point must be made about the Spaniards. Though their destruction of the inhabitants of the West Indies was a nightmare of human savagery, as was much of what they did in Central and South America, along with the iron-hard conquerors came noble men like Fa-

Below: A photograph of 20th century Zuñi Indians of New Mexico performing a Rain Dance.
Opposite page: The Zuñis, a tribe of Pueblo Indians, also had their Buffalo Dances. This print, made in 1854, shows a Zuñi brave costumed to begin a dance.

ther Las Casas and his successors, who believed in Indian rights and railed against their oppressors. Thanks to them, the enslavement of Indians was banned, and even proud conquistadors could be tried for cruelty. Of course, the human misery went on, but the Spanish record is shot through with beacons of light and humanity. Humanity was not to be much in evidence among the Anglo-Americans.

FAREWELL
TO THE EAST

'When I passed the last detachment of those suffering exiles and thought that my native countrymen had thus expelled them from their native soil and their much loved homes, and that too in this inclement season of the year, I turned from the sight with feelings which language cannot express and "wept like childhood then." '

So wrote 'A Native of Maine' in a New York paper in 1839 about his glimpse of the Cherokee on their journey to Indian Territory, leaving their beloved homeland forever. In all, some 60,000 Indians of the Five Civilized Tribes—Cherokee, Creek, Choctaw, Chickasaw and Seminoles—were exiled in a series of Trails of Tears, a direct result of a frontiersman, Andrew Jackson, being elected President in 1828. Here is how it happened.

The story of the Indians repeated itself down the centuries: the arrival of the white man, often welcomed; growing tensions, usually over land; the wars which whites almost always won in the end; and disease, liquor and despair. No doubt the ancestors of that undeniably humane man from Maine had been less emotional when it came to clearing Indians from the Atlantic seaboard in the north.

The French record is the best, for they were principally interested in the fur trade, not in land or in colonization. They married Indian women. Both trappers and priests learned Indian languages. Two years before the first English colony was established at Jamestown, Virginia in 1607, a French trading post was set up at Port Royal, Acadia (now Nova Scotia). The place was chosen by Samuel de Champlain, one of New France's (Canada's) greatest heroes. In the end, New France fell to the English because of lack of troops and lack of support from home, but Champlain hardly helped matters by making an enemy of the mighty Iroquois Confederacy.

The Iroquois were rightly feared warriors, but they also had a remarkable gift for democratic government, much admired by Benjamin Franklin and other Americans. The Five Nations of the Confederacy (the Mohawk, Oneida, Onondaga, Cayuga and Seneca) lived in a key position in western and central New York, an area rich in waterways which enabled them to dominate the fur trade and to be courted by Europeans. In the 18th century they became the Six Nations, giving a home to the Tuscarora, who were suffering from the oppression of whites in the Carolinas.

Champlain turned the Iroquois against France when, with two other Frenchmen, he was out with a Huron war party. His object was exploration, but the Huron were enemies of the Iroquois and a clash with a band of Mohawk was won by the Frenchmen's use of firearms, which killed three chiefs. This led to enduring hostility between the French and the Iroquois, with few periods of neutrality. Hostility grew worse when captive Iroquois were sent to be galley slaves in the Mediterranean. The Iroquois alliance with the English, a reasonably constant one, had its beginnings in that small forest incident.

To the south, the English colony of Jamestown managed to survive a series of crises and disasters, not least because of the aid given by the enchanting young Indian woman, Pocahontas. Not only did she save the life of the colony's most determined leader, Captain John Smith, when her father Powhatan was about to have him killed (some cynics believe that Smith made up the story) but also by marrying John Rolfe and becoming the ancestor of many distinguished Americans, she decisively helped the two races to coexist. Sad to say, she died in England, just as she was about to return home from her triumphs at the Court of King James I and elsewhere.

Soon the Indians found themselves under more and more pressure from the English, primarily because tobacco, the key crop being raised, used up land quickly and more was needed. So a reasonably harmonious atmosphere, especially among the older settlers, was transformed into hostility which led to war. Too late, the Powhatans rebelled in 1622. Already the colonists' population had swelled enough to take a terrible revenge on the Indians whose numbers had been reduced by disease.

Meanwhile, two years earlier the Pilgrim Fathers had landed to the north on Cape Cod. Intensely religious, they were helped by the local Indians, without whom they might have starved. The same basic sequence of events occurred, the war in this case, 'King Philip's War,' breaking out in 1675. After the defeat of the In-

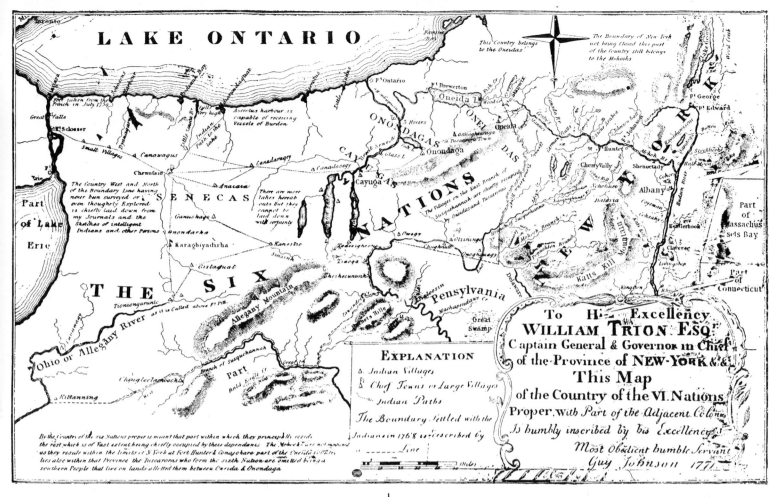

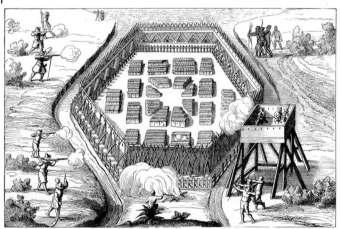

Top: A map of 1771 by Guy Johnson showing the territory of the Six (Indian) Nations of the Confederacy.

Above right: Champlain attacking an Iroquois fort. Above left: An old print of Champlain attacking an Indian village.

dian confederacy led by Metacom, King Philip, of the Wampanoag, hundreds of Indians were sent as slaves to the West Indies, including Philip's wife and child. That child was the grandson of the 'noble Massasoit' who had done so much to help the Pilgrims. Reverend Increase Mather, some of whose sayings on the subject of the Indian dead deserve a place in an anthology of bestiality, made one significant statement about what Philip's reaction must have been on hearing about the capture of his family: 'It must be bitter as death for him to lose his wife and only son, for the Indians are marvellously fond and affectionate towards their children.'

Philip was killed soon after the loss of his family. As for Mather's gleeful remark, the chief is said to have exclaimed on hearing the news of his loss: 'My heart breaks; now I am ready to die . . .'

During the holocaust unleashed by the Indians, Rogers Williams of Rhode Island, who

There were times when Indians attacked settlers without provocation. This is an Iroquois slaughter.

Top: Iroquois warriors attacking American settlers. Above: American colonists warding off an attack of the Iroquois. Above right: Seventeenth century combat.

had been banished from Massachusetts for championing religious tolerance and, equally out-of-line, Indian land rights, was spared, along with his colony. He and William Penn, who made a treaty with the Delaware in 1682, were famous exceptions to the rule of hostility. Yet many ordinary whites and Indians, even in desperate times, enjoyed genuine friendships.

The Dutch proved that they could commit atrocities as heinous as any. On Staten Island in 1643, where Wappinger who had asked for protection were slaughtered, a Hackensack was tortured in front of a laughing governor in a manner that equalled the Iroquois at their cruelest. The victim was even fed his own flesh. Fiendish as Indian torture could be, they at least had respect for the valiant.

There was never any real hope of the Indians throwing the whites into the Atlantic except, perhaps, in the earliest days. The settlers would have come again anyway. However, in the 1760s there was a rebellion that might have driven the English back to the coast for a time, at least.

The French had by now lost Canada. Too few in numbers, they had long ago lost their main Indian allies, the Huron, who had been destroyed as a major power by the Iroquois in 1649.

Before the French and Indian War (known as the Seven Years' War in Canada) broke out in 1756, the Indians and some Frenchmen had won a devastating victory against General Braddock's army in the forests of Pennsylvania. This was followed by other successes, but Wolfe's victory at Quebec in 1759 and Amherst's at Montreal in 1760 saw the end of New France.

One reason for the British victory was the refusal once again of the Iroquois to help the French. They stayed loyal partly because of the skill of William Johnson. This genial Irishman liked acquiring land but also genuinely liked Indians. As trader, then as 'Colonel of the Six Nations', finally as superintendent of all Indian affairs in the north, he was one of the most influential men in America. He became Sir William for his services at the Battle of Lake George in 1755, Britain's only victory that grim year, achieved by some 3000 Colonists and 300 Iroquois, mostly Mohawk. Johnson's charm even disarmed the fanatically religious New Englanders, when, before the battle, he did a war dance with his Indian friends. Yet it was all even he could do to keep the Iroquois loyal when the Ottawa chief, Pontiac, led his rebellion in 1763. In fact, the Seneca, the most westerly tribe of the Iroquois, joined Pontiac for a time.

Pontiac's aim was to bring back the French as well as drive the English back over the Alleghenies. Fort after fort fell to the Indians, who, just for once, were truly united. But the fort at Detroit held, and Pontiac gradually lost control of his many different tribes. The great rebellion faded and collapsed.

Now, with the French menace ended, it was only a matter of time before the Colonists rebelled against England, whose policies were guaranteed to provoke rebellion. Yet on the frontier, Britain's policy was honorable. There was a genuine attempt to keep Americans out of Indian territory. They drew the Proclamation Line of 1763, which aimed to keep the Colonists east of the watershed of the Alleghenies. But it infuriated both Virginian land companies and the growing number of people who wished to head westward.

When the American Revolution broke out in 1775, both sides trying to enlist Indian aid, the British having more success, probably because Sir William Johnson had died the previous

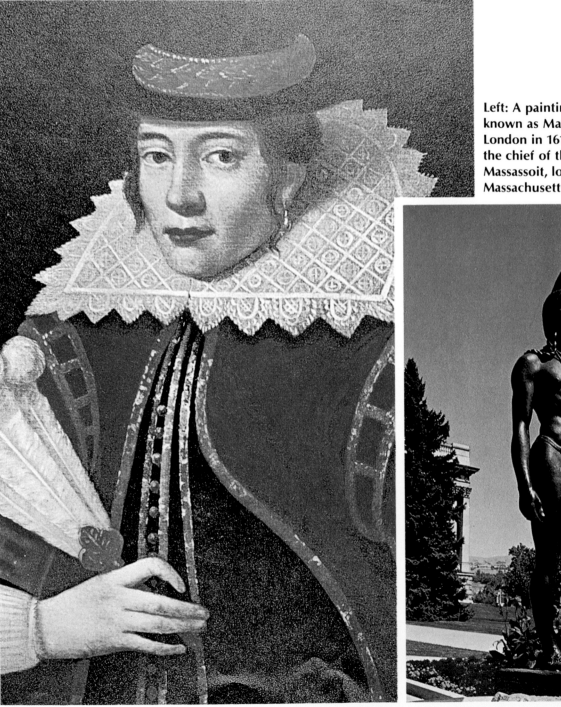

Left: A painting of Pocahontas (also known as Matoaks) when she was in London in 1616. Below: A statue of the chief of the Wampanoag, Massassoit, located in Plymouth, Massachusetts.

year. Now, though his son, Sir John, and other members of his family, were key members of the Loyalist side in New York, the leading figure on the northern frontier was Joseph Brant (Thayendanegea) the war chief of the Six Nations.

Brant was the younger brother of Molly Brant, Johnson's last Mohawk mistress, regarded, however, by everyone as his wife. Frontier opinion, and portraits, suggest that Brant may have been Johnson's son by another Indian woman, and Sir William certainly saw to it that he was well educated. As a youth he had fought in the French and Indian War; now

he was the leading Indian figure in New York. Even his influence could not prevent the Iroquois, the Tuscarora, and the Oneida from siding mainly with the Rebels, the Onondaga remaining generally neutral. Brant went to London in 1775–76 to be sure that a British alliance would safeguard Indian land rights. Boswell interviewed him, Romney painted him, and he made a deep impression on all who met him. Satisfied, he returned to America, fought on Long Island where he made a lifelong friend in Lord Hugh Percy, later second Duke of Northumberland and an honorary Mohawk, then penetrated north to his people.

Below: Osceola, the chief of the Seminoles. Right: Joseph Brant (also known as Thayendanegea), the chief of the Mohawk Indians, as painted by George Romney, c. 1776.

Though many tribes fought with the British in the war, only Brant and his Iroquois had it in their power to change its course. The fertile Mohawk valley, once Brant's home, was Washington's army's breadbasket, and the Indians and Tory Loyalists virtually destroyed it. The hardiest of the surviving settlers hung on until Washington had troops to spare to ravage the Iroquois homeland. But the final blow came when the Iroquois were left out of the peace treaty of 1783. They split, some remained in New York, and Brant led the rest to the Grand River in what is now Ontario, where today their descendants live just outside Brantford. Brant paid an even more spectacular visit to London in 1786, once again to secure his people's rights. Like Pontiac, and like Tecumseh after him, he had a vision of an Indian front united against the Americans, but he had to content himself with his smaller world in Canada, where, as an Iroquois and an officer in the British Army, his loyalties were divided. President Washington personally offered him generous rewards to help effect peace in the Northwest, but American peace usually meant loss of Indian land. The offer was rejected.

Finally, after the United States Army had been utterly defeated on the northern frontier in 1791 and 1792, the Americans won a great victory at Fallen Timbers in 1794. Now the days of the Indians in the Northwest were numbered.

Early in the nineteenth century, the great Shawnee, Tecumseh, became the last to try to unite the eastern tribes and hold the border, which was then the Ohio River. A magnificent orator and a man of rare stature and vision, his power over many different tribes had the Americans genuinely worried. Once again it seemed that the Indians might be truly united. General William Henry Harrison, governor of Indiana and a notable procurer of Indian lands, recognized the danger, but in 1811, when Tecumseh was absent, his messianic brother, known as the Prophet, launched a premature attack on Harrison at Tippecanoe which failed. He was discredited and Tecumseh's union was doomed. The next year, he decided to side with the British in the War of 1812. He helped destroy American chances of seizing Canada, but was killed at the Battle of the Thames in 1813.

Top: An Ottawa Indian and his family going to war. Above: An 18th century drawing of an Iroquois chief holding an enemy scalp. Below: Joseph Brant's grandfather, Sa Ga Yeath Qua Pieth Ton, one of the four Iroquois chiefs who visited England in the year 1710.

Top left: An Iroquois council house. Above far left: Tribal warfare depicted on a tepee skin. Above right: A council of Huron Indian chiefs.
Above center: Billy Bowlegs (Halpatter-Micco) of the Seminoles. Left: Joseph Brant (1742-1807) of the Mohawks. Below left: A painting by Remington—*Fur Trapper and Indian Shake Hands.* Below: Smith and Pocahontas.

King Powhatan comands C. Smith to be flayne, his daughter Pokahontas beggs his life his thankfullnes and how he Subieoled 39 of their kings read & history

After that, the idea of a single united Indian nation, always an impossible dream, crumbled away forever.

By the 1830s, with the sad campaign called Black Hawk's War, the Indians were finally driven westward, the only ones left in the old Northwest being a few scattered bands located around the Great Lakes. Tribes, some still remembered, some of them forgotten, had fought and had lost and were banished from the East forever, tribes whose very names—Delaware, Miami and the rest—are like tunes of vanished glories.

The most notorious of all these enforced removals were those of the Five Civilized Tribes. They had a long and complicated relationship with the white powers—England, Spain, France and, finally, the United States—which tried to dominate the South. They had often fought against each other. Their civilizations ad-

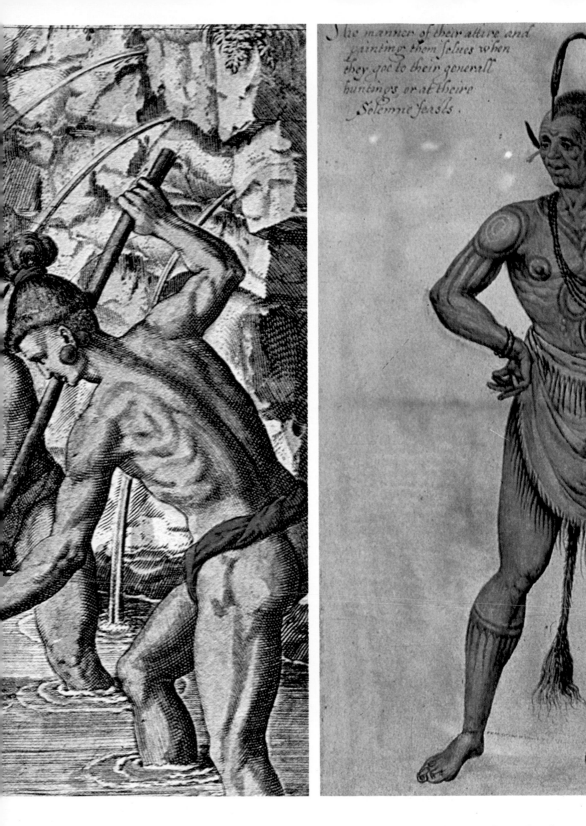

The manner of their attire and
painting them selues when
they goe to their generall
huntings or at theire
Solemne feasts.

Left: An engraving of 1591 by Theodor de Bry, *Florida Indians Washing for Gold.* **Right: A tattooed chief of North Carolina c 1585.**

vanced swiftly in the early years of the 19th century, none more so than that of the Cherokee. Their government was modeled on the United States government, while thanks to Sequoya's alphabet, the Cherokee rapidly became literate, even publishing a newspaper in 1828. Their chief was the remarkable John Ross, to-tally identified with them, though only one-eighth Indian.

The Creeks, too, had an extraordinary leader, Alexander McGillivray, at a time when the Creek and Seminoles were one nation. He died in 1796, having established himself as a diplomat of genius in his crafty dealings with Americans, British and Spaniards. Andrew Jackson, who had been well served by Indian troops in his time, and whose lands he then managed to

Top left: The death of Tecumseh. Above left: The defeat of the Sac and the Fox in the Battle of Bad Axe. Above right: A Virginia Indian Village, 1590. Opposite above: Sequoya's Cherokee alphabet. Below: John Ross, the Cherokee leader.

A Florida Indian dwelling and canoe of 1564 by Theodore de Bry.

A modern Seminole Indian family in Florida. They are cooking corn fritters.

reduce, started work on his Indian Removal Bill almost as soon as he became President in 1828. It needed the cooperation of the states concerned to facilitate his plans, but Georgia, Alabama and Mississippi were only too eager to help. The Cherokee, by now some of the most prosperous citizens in the United States, were well and truly doomed when gold was found on their land. The matter reached the Supreme Court and John Marshall, the Chief Justice, decided that Georgia had no right to the Cherokee lands. He spoke passionately, but Jackson said: 'John Marshall has made his decision; now let him enforce it.'

So it came about that the Five Civilized Tribes were herded to Indian Territory, the

CHEROKEE ALPHABET.

CHARACTERS SYSTEMATICALLY ARRANGED WITH THE SOUNDS

a	e	i	o	oo	v
ga	ka	ge	gi	go	gu	gv
ha		he	hi	ho	hu	hv
la		le	li	lo	lu	lv
ma		me	mi	mo	mu	
na	hna	nah	ni	no	nu	nv
qua		que	qni	quo	quu	quv
s	sa	se	si	so	su	sv
da	ta	de	t	di	ti	do	du	dv
dla	tla	tle	cle	tlo	tlu	tlv
tsa		tse	tsi	tso	tsu	tsv
wa		we	wi	wo	wu	wv
ya		ye	yi	yo	yu	yv

SOUNDS REPRESENTED BY VOWELS

A as a in father, or short as a in rival.
E as a in hate, or short as e in met.
I as i in pique, or short as i in pin.
O as o in note, but as approaching to aw in law.
U as oo in moon, or short as u in pull.
V as u in but, nasalized.

CONSONANT SOUNDS.

G, is sounded hard approaching to k; sometimes before e, i, u and v, its sound is k. D has a sound between the English d and t; sometimes, before o, u, and v its sound is t; when written before l and s the same analogy prevails

All other letters as in English.

Syllables beginning with g, except ga have sometimes the power of k; syllables when written with tl, except tla sometimes vary to dla.

amount of cruelty involved in these Trails of Tears varying from place to place and tribe to tribe. At their worst they shamed humanity. It is absurd to misunderstand the reason for anti-Indian feeling on the frontier, especially when the wars were at their height and atrocity was breeding atrocity, but these tribes in the 1830s were much more admirable citizens than most of those who wanted them out. Only the Seminoles, helped by the place they chose for their heroic stand, the Everglades of Florida, put up serious resistance to the inevitable.

The First Seminole War (1816–18) took place when Florida was still Spanish. Runaway slaves fled there and joined the Indians. Jackson marched in, defeated the Indians and prepared the ground for Florida's incorporation into the Union. The Second Seminole War (1835–42) broke out when the Indians refused to go west. Hellish for the troops involved, the war was an epic of endurance, even by Indian standards. While a few unfortunate Indians were taken to Indian Territory when captured, the rest, under Osceola, a chief of storybook nobility, kept up a ferocious struggle against soldiers, sailors and bloodhounds. At a conference in 1835, Osceola was treacherously seized, and he died in prison. His comrade Wild Cat, with 16 warriors and two women, made an incredible escape from the fort at St Augustine through a small hole 18 feet from the floor. Meanwhile, in the Everglades mothers killed their small children so as to fight with the men.

Finally, the Americans had had enough. Those Seminoles who wanted to stay were allowed to do so. Some, without actually fighting, remained officially at war with the United States, and not until 1962 did they resume relations with the nation that failed to defeat them.

One other group survives to this day in the East. A few hundred Cherokee escaped one of the Trails of Tears by hiding out in the mountains of North Carolina. Their descendants—some 4500 of them—have not intermarried with other groups, unlike the Cherokee of Oklahoma. In a special amphitheater in their beautiful reservation, visitors can see the most famous of all dramas staged by Indians about their past, *Unto These Hills*. For the Cherokee of North Carolina, unlike so many of today's Indians, past and present are happily united.

A painting by Charles M Russell showing some Comanche Indian braves returning from a horse stealing raid.

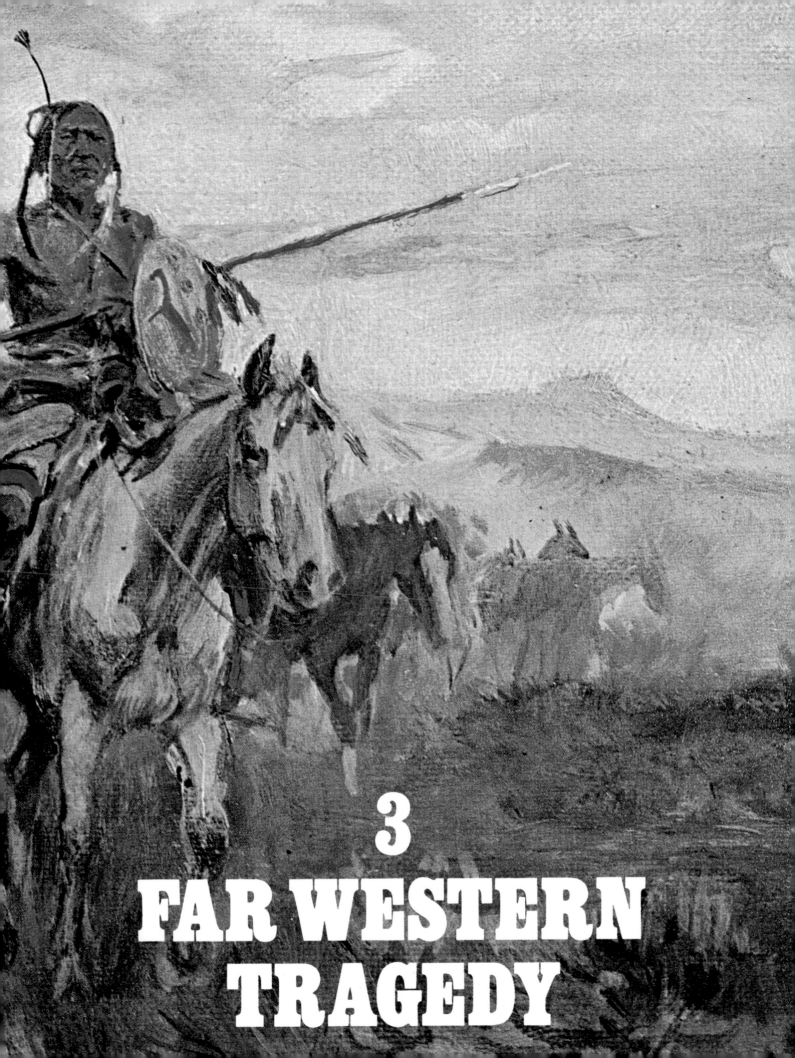

3
FAR WESTERN
TRAGEDY

'Gold! Gold! Gold from the American River!' That cry, shouted in the main street of the small town of San Francisco on 15 May, 1848 by an extrovert Mormon named Sam Brannan, gave away the secret of James Marshall's gold strike at Sutter's Mill the previous January. It was a cry that was to reverberate round the world, bring hundreds of thousands of people to California, and spell the doom of its Indians.

California, so soon to be known as the Golden State, had a larger Indian population than any other area of similar size in North America. In terms of art, agriculture and social organization, the vast number of small groups seen by Europeans from the 16th century onward were among the least developed of all Indians. Though some of those who lived in the deserts of Utah and Nevada were still less developed. Yet California's Indians seem to have been happy enough. There was no shortage of food and the climate varied from pleasant to idyllic. Only the Mohave and the Yuma who lived in the southeastern region were in the least organized, and only the Yuma were farmers. The rest led a mainly peaceful and dream-like existence. The few visitors from European ships found the natives they met both friendly and happy.

Not until 1769 did Spain move into California—Upper California as it was known then. A Russian threat from the north was the reason for the migration. Along with garrisons came the famous Californian missions, 21 of them in all, staffed by Franciscan priests.

Considering what was to happen later, the missions stand out as the reasonably humane institutions they were certainly meant to be. But in fact, only the coastal Indians were influenced by the missions, and, instead of their old, carefree life, they found themselves working hard at every sort of trade, including outdoor activities like farming, which must have seemed singularly pointless. The priests tried to turn them into good Catholics, punished them with the lash if they misbehaved, and let them out occasionally in groups to collect fruit and potential converts. Many of the priests were fine, dedicated men, but they were at best benevolent despots as far as their charges were concerned. Laughing faces became sullen. The missions succeeded but their workers lost that simple happiness noticed by earlier travelers.

What would have happened if Spain had remained the ruler of California can only be guessed at. It would certainly have been infinitely better for the Indians than what did happen.

Mexico broke away from Spain in 1821 and the missions were made secular in 1834. At least the Indians had had security under the Spanish priests, but now the Mexican liberators grabbed the missions and the spoils in a way Henry VIII would have recognized, with the result that huge ranchos were formed.

Already the Indian population was shrinking. From 1800 to 1850, it slumped from 260,000 to 100,000. This was not deliberate genocide—that came later—but was simply caused by new diseases and new ways of life. Even the conquest of California by Americans in 1846 was not in itself a prelude to disaster, but the finding of gold on the American River was; and ironically, it was found just over a week before the official peace treaty between Mexico and the United States made California American.

A single statistic without embellishment sums up the story. By 1900, there were only 15,000 Indians left alive in California. It is reckoned that as early as 1859 there were only 30,000 left.

Only a minority of the many thousands of whites from the eastern United States and other parts of the world who poured into California had the remotest interest in, or sympathy for, the native population. And it hardly helped the Indians that, unlike so many tribes elsewhere, they were nearly all peace-loving with no warrior tradition. The southern Californian Indians, far from the goldfields, suffered less, in the sense that many of them survived in however debauched a state. But further north, Indians were hunted down like animals, killed or enslaved, their women raped and often forced into prostitution, their children brought up in bondage. The only reason that they were not wiped out altogether was that there were too many of them. The map of California is dotted with small reservations where some of their descendants live today.

There was only one genuine war in California, fought along the border with Oregon. It

Above: Lewis and Clark being guided by
Sacagawea—a detail of a painting by E S Paxon in
the State Capitol in Helena, Montana. Right: An
early engraving of a Jesuit missionary preaching to
some of the California Indians.

Below: The Spaniards brought Christianity to the
Indians of the West Coast. Here the recessional
after a Roman Catholic service at a California
mission has broken up a card game, but the
Indians at the right remain pious.

Above: A scene of an Indian family on the move. Each of the horses at the right is pulling a travois loaded with household goods. Right: A maiden of the Blackfoot tribe, painted by N H Hardy.

was a valiant one, but marred by a brutal, foolish murder at a time when the Indians concerned needed all the moral support they could get.

These Indians were the Modoc. They lived in the Tule Lake country, and in the 1850s they found their best land being annexed by the whites. Unlike so many Californian Indians, the Modoc were prepared to fight back, but a young chief called Kintpuash decided to try and get along with the intruders. He liked their way of life, and the two races settled down on reasonably amicable terms. The Americans gave a number of the Modoc new names, Kintpuash acquiring the name by which he is remembered today—Captain Jack.

In the Civil War period, relations deteriorated and the whites managed to get the Modoc moved to the Klamath Reservation in Oregon, where they found themselves regarded as interlopers. Worse, supplies reached the Klamath from the government, but none came for the Modoc. So Captain Jack and his people went

Right: The Whitman Mission in 1845. Dr Marcus Whitman was killed here by the Cayuse in 1847.

Below: A Comanche warrior as painted by George Catlin. With his spear, shield, bow and arrows, he is fully prepared to go into battle to protect the tepees in the background.

A 20th century photograph of a modern Nez Percé Indian in full battle regalia astride his mustang.

Above: The United States Army pursued the Nez Percé Indians for more than a thousand miles.

home. The authorities there were prepared to allow them to stay, but the local settlers were not. Naturally, evil reports were circulated about Jack and his people, and, finally, the tribe was ordered to return to Oregon. In November, 1872, Captain James Jackson at the head of B Troop, First Cavalry, headed out of Fort Klamath for the Modoc home on Lost River.

A tense confrontation occurred, with Jackson ordering Captain Jack and his men to lay down their arms. They did so, with the exception of Scarface Charley (another white nickname), who drew his pistol on Jackson. Both men fired and both were unharmed. Meanwhile the Modoc rushed for their pile of arms and a fight commenced, ending after half an hour with the flight of the Indians. Jackson claimed that 'not less than 16' of the 'worst' of them were dead, though, in fact, only one was, as was one of his own men.

The families of Jack's band paddled along the river leading to Lake Tule while their men

marched along the bank. The band led by Hooker Jim was attacked by ranchers, who were beaten back, and the two groups met each other in lava beds below the lake, which were to be known as Captain Jack's Stronghold, and which are now a National Monument.

This natural fortress, well known to the Indians, had just enough grass for the cattle the Modoc brought with them, while the lake would provide water. Into the fortress came some 250 Modoc, probably not more than 60 of them warriors. Captain Jack was alarmed that Hooker Jim had killed local whites whom the Indians knew. He had hoped to be left in peace in the stronghold, but realized that war was now inevitable.

The soldiers arrived on 13 January 1873 and a reconnaissance party was driven away from a bluff. On the 16th, 225 regulars and 104 volunteers appeared. It seems that Jack decided there was no point in fighting if it meant the destruction of his people, but he was outvoted. Natu-

This is a detail from a painting by Charles Schreyrogel.

A photograph taken of the great chief of the Nez Percé tribe, Chief Looking Glass.

rally, those who had killed settlers wanted no surrender.

The first attack, complete with artillery, started the next day. It ended in failure, and the Indians went out and collected guns and ammunition from the dead. The whites rightly decided that they needed more troops and guns.

The commander of the Department of the Columbia, General Canby, a humane and popular man, came to take personal control of the embarrassing little war. Already there had been peace feelers, carried to Jack by his cousin Winema, who was married to a white man, Frank Riddle. The Americans were offering a reservation in the Southwest, away from possible trial in a hostile Oregon. Hooker Jim was so impressed that he and eight followers actually surrendered to the peace commissioners. These were Alfred Meacham, once the Modoc agent in Oregon, L S Dyar from the Klamath Reservation, and Reverend Eleasar Thomas, a Methodist. Unfortunately, an Oregonian spotted the

Modoc, made some pointed remarks about the dead settlers, and the Indians escaped as fast as they could to the safety of the stronghold.

Jack was soon in an intolerable situation, for it was announced that he and his band could come in safety, but that Hooker Jim and his men could not. Despite a friendly meeting with Canby, more and more troops arrived. By April there were to be 1000 of them. Canby kept trying to resolve the crisis peacefully and several meetings took place in no-man's-land, but always the question of Hooker Jim and his men prevented a solution from being found.

After one bitter council in the stronghold, Winema, sent in by Canby to tell Jack that any who wished to surrender to him could come out with her, was stopped by a relative. He warned her that Hooker Jim's faction was prepared to kill anyone who opposed them, including white men, at any future meeting. Her husband passed on the warning to the peace commissioners, but it was written off as a mere

Probably the greatest leader of the Nez Percé Indians—Chief Joseph. Inset: Another photograph taken of Chief Joseph at the end of his career. His Indian name was Hinmaton-Yalaktit, or Thunder Rolling in the Mountains.

threat. Hooker Jim, however, meant what he said. At the climax of another angry council, he told Jack that unless he killed Canby at their next meeting, he would be killed by his own people. Jack told him it would be the act of a coward to kill Canby, but Hooker Jim said it would be a brave act in front of the soldiers. Women's clothes were draped over Jack's shoulders and he was jeered at and disowned by his opponents, who later were so foully to betray him. Finally, he gave in and said he would kill the general.

An English-speaking Modoc, Boston Charley, went to Canby and asked for a meeting to be held on 11 April—Good Friday. The Modoc would be unarmed and so should the commissioners be.

Jack made one more plea to his opponents, but was outvoted again. Finally, they decided that if Canby would agree to the Modoc terms, he would not be killed. The terms were the granting of a reservation nearby and the removal of the troops before peace talks. Jack had told the council what would happen if Canby were killed, but it made no difference. The countdown to tragedy had begun.

The council tent stood midway between the stronghold and the headquarters of Colonel Gillem, First Cavalry. It had been erected a few days earlier in case of sudden storms. The Indians arrived first: Jack, Hooker Jim, and four other Modoc, all with pistols under their coats. They built a sagebrush fire, as the day was chilly. Then the commissioners arrived: Canby, Thomas, Meacham, and Dyar, also Frank Riddle and Winema, who was known as Toby to the whites. Riddle was Canby's official interpreter. With them also were Boston Charley and Bogus Charley, who had been sent ahead to the white men's camp. They both had rifles over their shoulders; Dyar and Meacham carried concealed derringers.

Canby made a friendly speech, promising a good country where the Modoc could live like white people. Jack said he did not want to leave the Modoc country, but live on a reservation between the lake and the lava beds. Also the soldiers must go away before any peace talks.

Meacham now said that any Modoc who wanted to, could stay in the lava beds until a new reservation was found, while Hooker Jim took Meacham's coat from his saddle and donned it, saying: 'You think I look like Meacham.' To lower the tension, Meacham offered his hat as well. 'You keep a while,' said Hooker Jim. 'Hat will be mine by and by.'

Canby pointed out that only the President could send the troops away. After a few more exchanges, Jack suddenly shouted in Modoc: 'All ready,' drew his pistol and killed Canby. Boston Charley killed Thomas, but Meacham was saved when Winema knocked the pistol aside. The other commissioner, Dyar, escaped with the Riddles. General Sherman wired Canby's immediate superior, General Schofield: 'Any measure of severity to the savages will be sustained.' He had the nation behind him. Meanwhile, Colonel Gillem, with Canby's death the senior officer on the spot, began working his way toward the stronghold, the attacks beginning on 15 April with a new, grim earnestness. On the third day, the troops entered the stronghold only to find that the enemy had vanished.

Terino Indian scouts found them again, but the 64-strong army reconnaissance force that went in to check their new defensive position was humiliatingly ambushed. Half the patrol ran away and of the courageous rest, 25 were killed and 16 were wounded.

The new commander, General Jefferson C Davis, made some strong remarks about the quality of his enlisted men, but he was an able commander, and by mid-May, he had more troops and had managed to raise the morale of his shaky command. However, when he moved in on the Modoc positions, the enemy had vanished once more.

This was not a strategic withdrawal by a united force. The Modoc had broken up into small bands. Hooker Jim with 13 men and their families had deserted the leader whose inevitable destruction he had caused, then, despicably, he surrendered to Davis and offered to find Jack in return for amnesty. The turncoats tracked down Jack and urged him to surrender. He told them to go back to the whites. If they came near him, he would shoot them like curs. But, finally and inevitably, he was caught, dressed in what was left of Canby's uniform. 'Jack's legs gave out,' he said. 'I am ready to die.'

After a trial in language they little understood, Captain Jack, Schonchin John, Boston Charley and Black Jim were hanged. Hooker Jim was one of those who gave evidence against them.

Jack's courage held to the end. When a settler shouted to him as the rope was being adjusted round his neck: 'Jack! What would you give me to take your place?', he flashed back: '500 ponies and both my wives!'

Jack's body was dug up the night after the hanging and was soon appearing in the East at carnivals at 10 cents a look.

Robert A Murray, historian of the Modoc War, notes that considering the number of Indians involved in hostilities, this was the most expensive Indian war that the United States ever fought. It was also the only war in which an army general was killed by Indians.

One hundred fifty-three Modoc were sent to Indian Territory, where Hooker Jim died. In 1909, those survivors who wished to, were allowed to return to the Northwest and settle on the Klamath Reservation in Oregon.

An additional casualty of the expensive and humiliating war was President Grant's Peace Policy. This dated back to 1868 and advocated the concentration of Indians, civilizing and educating them, and getting them to become self-sufficient in feeding themselves. The war, especially the slaying of Canby and Thomas, made the very word peace suspect, despite the fact that the causes of the war had precious little to do with anything but local white mismanagement of and hostility toward a small group of people. In the public and official mind, however, it was now even more fully established that Indians could not be trusted. As a result, such peace policy as there was became to signify peace for Indians on the reservation and war for those off it.

In the Great Basin country of Nevada and Utah, between the Sierra Nevada and the Rockies, lived peoples whose life-styles were even simpler than those of California's Indians. Most spoke variations of the Shoshonean language, and some, like the Gosiute, or Diggers, beside the Great Salt Lake, were perhaps the most primitive Indians in America. Yet cousins of these desert dwellers, the Shoshones of Wyoming, led the stirring life of the Plains Indians.

There were Ute in Utah and Colorado, Paiute on the Nevada-Utah border; there were Bannock—mountain Paiute—in Idaho, and Klamath, whom we have already briefly met, in Oregon, and a wealth of tribes in northern Oregon and Washington. Above all, there were the Nez Percé.

The Diggers were too poor to cause anyone much trouble, and their land was too barren for them to be exterminated on account of it. They therefore remained. The Paiute were more daring. A frontier mob, 105 strong, whose slogan was 'An Indian for breakfast and a pony to ride', attacked Paiute at Pyramid Lake after an incident which seems to have begun with the raping of two Indian women. The Indians won, but, as inevitably happened, lost the short war that followed. Otherwise, the main Paiute claim to historical fame is their racing after Pony Express riders.

The Northern Shoshones have a greater claim to fame. The Comanche, the lords of the

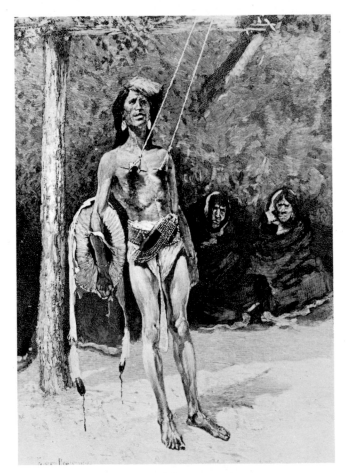

A Blackfoot Indian youth undergoing the ordeal of the Sun Dance—a ritual which he must suffer in order to become a warrior. Opposite: Tomochichi of the Yamacraw Creek Indians, with his son.

The Great Modoc Indian leader, Kintpuash, also
known as Having the Water Brush, but best known
as Captain Jack.

Kintpuash was one of the commanders in the
Medoc War of 1872-73. He was hanged at Ft
Klamath on 3 October 1873.

south plains, were a breakaway branch of the tribe, but the Shoshones who remained were famous in their own right. Lewis and Clark's much admired guide, Sacagawea, was a Shoshone. Arguments have raged as to how useful—as opposed to how delightful—she was, but the fact that Lewis and Clark had an Indian woman with them on their great expedition to the Pacific and back (1804-06) undoubtedly helped allay the fears of watching Indians, and she was able to be of considerable service when she reached her own tribe; she had been kidnapped from them some years earlier. The Shoshones helped the party head westward.

Later, the Shoshones, under their great Chief Washakie, who died in his nineties in 1900, were to be good friends of the whites. They helped settlers and—thanks to their long hostility to the Sioux and Cheyenne—helped the army on the plains. For that, certain writers have dubbed them mercenaries in the less pleasant sense of the word. In fact, they were allies against a common enemy and it is unhistorical to suggest otherwise, even if the 'hostiles' are now more widely admired by Indians and white men alike. The Pawnee served the whites for exactly the same reason.

The Indians of the Northwest—Joseph and his Nez Percé apart—are not often treated at any length except in specialized books. Only a few can be described here, yet their fate was as wretched as that of most tribes. They had obtained horses around 1700, and many lived along the Columbia River and its tributaries. The Yakima, who were also called Cayuse, became famous horse dealers—so much so that Oregonians started calling horses cayuses, and the term later spread through the West.

Though the great emigrations to Oregon did not start until 1843, they were originally triggered off by the reports of missionaries in Oregon, most notably the Methodist, Dr Jason Lee in 1834, and the Congregational minister, Dr Marcus Whitman in 1836. The thousands of Americans who crossed the plains and mountains made the Northwest American, not British as it might have been, by right of possession. Warlike noises were made by President Polk that the border between Canada and the United States be drawn at the 54th Parallel, but in 1846, it was settled at the 49th.

At first, there was little trouble between the Indians and the newcomers. There were only some 10,000 of them by the end of the 1840s, not to be compared in numbers or in character with the flood of Forty-Niners so soon to overwhelm California's tribes.

Whitman and his wife, Narcissa, settled with the Cayuse at their request. Their mission was near today's Walla Walla in southern Washington. The other missionaries, the Spaldings and William Gray, settled with the Nez Percé at Lapwai in Idaho.

After a good start, and with other missionaries coming West to join them, problems started to arise: a money shortage back in the East, a troublemaking missionary called Smith, and conversions to Catholicism being made by priests coming down from Hudson's Bay Company posts. 'Romanism stalks abroad,' said Mrs. Spalding. Its finest figure was Father de Smet, the Jesuit who spent many years with the Flathead and Coeur d'Alene Indians in Montana.

With the Protestant missions being threatened with closure—their officials in the East soon changed their minds—Whitman went back to report, returning with the great wagon train of 1843. Tension grew each year, and the Spaldings had to close their once successful mission school, partly because a Delaware who had married a Nez Percé was violently antimissionary. He felt this way because of the way his people had been treated in the East. Christianity seemed to him a sham.

The school closed in 1846 and that winter was a very severe one. Cruelly, the Cayuse suffered several hundred deaths from measles, many deaths being perhaps caused by their drastic attempt at a cure—a steam bath followed by a dip in cold water. Rumors spread that Whitman was poisoning Indians to take their lands, that missionaries and settlers were in league to that same end. The conversion battle between Catholics and Protestants hardly helped.

On 29 November 1847, the Cayuse struck the Whitman mission. It was a typically busy day. There were now many white assistants, also workers and children. Dr and Mrs Whitman were killed along with eleven other men, and women and children were taken prisoner, including the daughters of mountain men Jim Bridger and Joe Meek. Both girls, whose mothers were Indian, had measles and died of exposure.

Only the bravery of Mrs. Spalding and the good faith of a Nez Percé chief prevented another massacre at Lapwai. Though no friend of missionaries, the chief and his men helped the whites to escape.

Volunteers joined some Regulars to punish the Cayuse, and in 1850, to save the rest of the tribe, five of the Indians turned themselves in, after two years of hiding in the mountains. They were hanged. As so often happened, the wrong people—in this case, well-meaning friends of the Indians—had been attacked by those who rightly saw their way of life being threatened. And they had unwittingly chosen the worst possible time, with the country soon to be invaded by hordes of ex-Forty-Niners hoping to strike it rich further north. Worse still, Washington became a separate territory in 1853 under the governorship of a tough ex-army man, Isaac Stevens.

He was a keen railroad advocate—on his way to his new job he conducted a War Department Pacific Railway Survey—and he was soon pushing the idea of a northern transcontinental line. This, of course, would mean getting rid of awkward Indian land titles. After several small tribes west of the Cascade Mountains had been moved to reservations, he arranged for a major council to be held at Walla Walla. All the Indians of the upper Columbia River country who had had little or no contact with whites, were to attend.

The Council was held in May 1855 and the Indians were understandably suspicious. They had heard of the 'war' against the Rogue River Indians of southern Oregon waged by volunteers in 1853, which ended in the valley being 'bought' from the Indians for a trivial sum. In fact, the year after the Walla Walla Council, the Rogue River Indians were to rise again and be almost exterminated.

At Walla Walla were Yakima under their outstanding Chief Kamiakim, who had been trying to unite the tribes before the council started. There were also Nez Percé, Cayuse, Walla Walla and Umatilla. Stevens wanted them all to be placed on two reservations with

Opposite above: Two Digger, or Paiute, Indians of Nevada. Below: Beavers were important to Indians as a source of fur and food. This is the culmination of a beaver hunt.

the Nez Percé and Yakima. This idea was firmly rejected. Finally, after much bitter negotiating, vast areas of land were ceded by the Indians in return for reservations of their own choice, plus promises of goods and help in 'civilizing' their tribes.

Despite promises that the Indians could stay on their land until the various treaties were ratified by the Senate, Stevens at once allowed settlers into the treaty lands. Miners entered them, heading for strikes in British Columbia and northern Washington. The result was war, though it was never a war in the true sense of the word, but a series of outbreaks. The Nez Percé, keeping to their treaty, refused to join in, as did Chief Seattle of the Duwamish League of Puget Sound. The Yakima were the heart of the rebellion, even attacking river steamers. After his defeat, the great Kamiakan managed to escape to Canada. General Crook, later to be a famous fighter against the Apache and the Sioux, vividly described conditions in this little-known war in his *Autobiography:*

It was no infrequent occurrence for an Indian to be shot down in cold blood, or a squaw raped by some brute. Such a thing as a white man being punished for outraging an Indian was unheard of . . . The trouble with the army was that the Indians would confide in us as friends and we had to witness this unjust treatment of them without the power to help them. Then when they were pushed beyond endurance and would go on the war path we had to fight when our sympathies were with the Indians.

East of these unfortunate Indians were the Blackfoot Indians. The scourge of American mountain men, they were ready to trade with the British posts farther north. They were the only tribe to give real trouble to Lewis and Clark, and later American travelers suffered, too. Today, they live on both sides of the international border. Their worst experience of white hostility came in January 1870. The

Piegan were the most southerly tribe of the Blackfoot Confederacy. Major Eugene M Baker, with two squadrons of the Second Cavalry, virtually destroyed a Piegan village on the Marias River, killing 120 men and 53 women and children. There had been Indian depredations before, but, not for the first time, soldiers attacked the wrong camp. There was so much uproar in the East over the massacre that a move to transfer the Indian Department to the War Department was quashed. The wretched tribesmen, ravaged also by smallpox, were in no mood to renew the conflict.

Across the border, despite growing food shortages caused by the decimation of the buffalo herds, things were better ordered. It is only fair to note that there was never a settler versus Indian problem in the Canadian West, even when the wars were at their fiercest below the border. Given that, the North-West Mounted Police—tough and just, though paternalistic—were trusted by Indians in a way no law enforcement body, military or civilian, ever was below the border. The Mounties had been formed in 1873, and, in 1874, 300 scarlet-coated men marched westward. American whiskey-traders vanished from their outpost at Fort Whoop-up in what is now Alberta, and a treaty was made with the Blackfoot Indians under their great Chief, Crowfoot. 'If the police had not come to this country, where would we all be now?' he was to say later. 'Bad men and whiskey were killing us so fast that few of us would be left today.'

The late 1870s saw campaigns in the Northwest against other tribes, including the Bannock and 'renegade' Bannock, and the Shoshones known as Sheepeaters. The Bannock were joined by the Paiute in a war which, so General Crook later said, was caused by 'Hunger. Nothing but Hunger.' After long marches through rugged country and a number of battles, the Indians gave up the hopeless struggle.

Better known was the war against the Ute. Cattlemen and sheepherders like their Navaho enemies, they ranged widely in Utah and New Mexico. From the 1850s, they sided more often

California Indian women sorting acorns that have been brought in from the forests, from a painting by A A Jansson.

than not with the whites as auxiliaries. They had a good friend in Kit Carson, the ex-mountain man, and through him settled in western Colorado. There were some 3500 of them in six bands.

Ouray was their most influential chief. Bowing to the inevitable—there was a silver boom in the area, complete with a flood of miners—he ceded a quarter of the reservation. It was not enough for Coloradans, who wanted the Ute out altogether. They claimed that virtually every crime in Colorado was the work of the Ute. Ouray, who was seriously ill, could barely keep his people in check.

Fortunately for the Coloradans, they got a genuine atrocity to boost their desires in late 1879. At the White River Agency, there was an eccentric old agent, Nathan Meeker, who, among other ideas, had hoped to start a Utopian colony. He also had a dream in which 'his' Ute would be instantly civilized and become self-sufficient farmers. Tact was not in him and his charges were becoming mutinous.

He now demanded troops, but no one seemed to think that the matter was urgent. On 10 September, Chief Douglas beat him up and his urgent request for help was answered. Major Thornburgh, with a cavalry troop and a company of infantry, set out from Fort Steele, Wyoming, picking up more troops as he went. He soon had 153 soldiers and 25 civilians.

The enraged Indians, believing that they would be sent in chains to Indian Territory, met Thornburgh some 60 miles from the agency and told of their feelings about Meeker. Their leader was a fierce young brave called Jack.

Meeker, now very alarmed, agreed with the Ute plan to have Thornburgh advance to the agency with only five men, there to parley with the chiefs. Although the major agreed, he finally decided that his troops should be stationed near the agency. Naturally, the Ute felt they were being betrayed.

Thornburgh left the infantry and eight wagons behind and, with 120 troopers, crossed into the reservation. They came upon Jack with 100 warriors and, after some talk and a shot fired, perhaps by an Indian, a battle began. Thornburgh was killed and a fight lasted several hours, the Ute almost managing to burn out the troops by setting grass and sagebrush on fire. The new commander, Captain Payne, sent for help.

Fighting continued, and, on the 29th, the Ute killed Meeker and nine of his men and captured Mrs Meeker, her daughter Josephine and another woman and her two children. Mrs Meeker, Josephine and the other woman were raped.

The news of the battle brought troops by train and by road. Not until 5 October did the main relief force under Colonel Wesley Merrit arrive, and the Indians gave up the siege of Payne and his men. A few hours later, Merrit received a copy of a letter from Chief Ouray to the White River chiefs. In it, they were told to stop fighting as Jack and his band had agreed to do. Fearing the worst, Merrit marched to the White River agency and found the bodies.

News of the killings and the captives caused a national sensation. Troops were rapidly assembled and, finally, there were 1500 men in the field against the Ute. Despite bellicose statements from Generals Sherman and Sheridan, Carl Schurz, the wise and able Secretary of the Interior, decided that a major war would bring the rest of the Ute into action and result in the murder of the captives. He felt that Ouray's influence might prove decisive in getting the captives freed. Charles Adams, once a Ute agent, was asked to lead the peace mission and, despite military anger and fierce arguments among the Ute, he succeeded. It was a near thing, the tide being turned when Ouray's representative—the great Ute being ill—threatened on his leader's behalf to send the rest of the Ute nation against the White River hostiles.

The rebels were to go unpunished, it being decided that they had been forced to fight Thornburgh. However, an exception was made in the case of the 12 Indians judged to have been guilty of the killings and rapes at the agency. Yet it proved impossible to isolate the guilty Indians with the exception of Chief Douglas who was punished by being sent to Fort Leavenworth prison. His rape of Mrs Meeker was not mentioned publicly in order to avoid embarrassment to her.

The unfortunate Ute were punished by being driven into barren country in Utah. The only Ute, or, indeed, Indians, left in Colorado were the Southern Ute, who were given a narrow band of territory on the southwestern border of

Nathan Meeker, the Indian agent who was killed by the Utes of the White River Agency in September of the year 1879.

Josephine Meeker, who was captured and outraged in the Ute uprising in Colorado at the White River Agency in 1879.

the state that had once been home to other great tribes, including the Comanche, Kiowa, Cheyenne and Arapaho. Ouray died in 1880, aged 47, just before the final dispersal of his people.

Chief Joseph was a great leader of the Nez Percé. The story of his people's downfall starts with his father, also Joseph, who got his name from Reverend Spalding. Old Joseph was born a Cayuse, but he married a Nez Percé and became a member of a tribe that had welcomed Lewis and Clark and every white man after them. No Nez Percé had ever killed a white, and, in return, many whites deeply admired the handsome and intelligent Nez Percé.

Old Joseph attended the 1855 Walla Walla council. The Nez Percé treaty gave his band their old and beloved homeland in the Wallowa Valley, where Oregon, Idaho and Washington meet. Despite the appearance of miners who found gold, and the building of Lewiston,

the coming of settlers, and the ill-treatment of individual Nez Percé, the Indians kept the peace during the wars of the late 1850s.

Another council was held in 1863, giving the Wallowa Valley to the government and paving the way for settlers to move in. Old Joseph refused to sign this treaty and rightly raged against other chiefs who had never lived in the valley, but signed it away along with other tribal land. He tore up a New Testament that had been given to him and placed poles around the edges of his beloved domain. Meanwhile, settlers started moving into the land of the 'nontreaty' Indians, as they were called.

In 1871, Joseph died and his son, Young Joseph, took his place. His Indian name was Hinmaton-Yalaktit—Thunder Rolling in the Mountains—and he was about 30 years old.

Almost at once, he and his people were being ordered out of their valley by officials, but Joseph refused to budge. He asked for President Grant to intervene and, in June 1873, the Presi-

dent ordered part of the valley to stay in Nez Percé hands.

Commissioners arrived in the valley to organize a new Indian agency, but found that the Nez Percé wanted neither churches nor schools. Joseph made a subtle point when asked why he did not want the churches. 'They will teach us to quarrel about God,' he said, having had his fill of headhunters of various religious groups seeking converts.

It was too good to last. In 1875, the government went back on its word. Already settlers had come into the valley, followed by gold miners, who stole the tribes' magnificent horses and their cattle. Leading nontreaty Indians—White Bird, Looking Glass, Toohoolhoolzote, Eagle from the Light and others—argued with each other and Joseph over whether to fight now or try and live in peace. They decided to attempt the latter, but it was obvious that a single incident by an Indian or a settler could shatter the peace.

Back in 1874, the one-armed Civil War veteran, General Oliver Otis Howard, had become the commander of the Department of the Pacific. Known as the 'Christian General,' he had served after the war as head of the Freedmen's Bureau of the War Department for ex-slaves, and as founder and principal of a university for blacks in Washington, D.C. He had made peace with Cochise in 1872. Now he found himself sympathizing with the Nez Percé, but, as things turned out, he was not sympathetic enough. Remembering the Battle of the Little Bighorn in 1876, he feared an uprising in the Northwest. When an Indian was murdered by a settler, he decided to act, well-meaningly but cruelly.

A two-day council was held, the bemused Christian general quite failing to comprehend the Indians' love of their land. Worse, he confused it with a cult which was rampant among many of the tribes of the Northwest, known as the 'Dreamer' cult and militantly antiwhite. So Howard reported to the Government that if Joseph and his band were not moved to Lapwai by persuasion, force must be used.

Joseph decided that he must submit, but at a meeting in May 1877, he was given only 30 days to move. He pleaded that his stock could not be rounded up that quickly and that the Snake River was very high. Howard, whatever his private feelings may have been, was publicly unmoved.

Joseph and his subchiefs had no choice. Cavalry from Fort Walla Walla had already taken over the Wallowa Valley, and the Indians now gathered up their stock, Joseph being well aware that there was not enough room for it at Lapwai. The tribe gathered at Hell's Canyon on the Snake, which was turbulent from the spring rains. Young Nez Percé on their finest horses towed their people across on rafts, not one being lost. However, the next day many mares and cows, colts and calves, were swept down the river. The Indians joined other Nez Percé, the Salmon River bands of Chiefs Toohoolhoolzote and White Bird, and settled on Camas Prairie below the reservation boundary to put off the move to Lapwai for the ten remaining days before the deadline expired.

Naturally, the braves were split on the subject of future action, or inaction, then, on 13 June, three youths, bolstered by whiskey, killed four white men who were notorious for their bad treatment of Indians. Joseph and his brother Ollokot tried to calm their people, saying that they would explain to Howard, but they had lost their hold on the younger warriors, 16 of whom rode off and killed 14 or 15 whites, then went on an orgy of drinking and looting.

There could be no turning back now. Chief Joseph later said that he would have given his own life if he could have undone the killing of the white men. He blamed his young men and the whites. 'I would have taken my people to the buffalo country Montana without fighting, if possible.'

So the heroic 1700-mile march began over some of the most rugged terrain in North America. At the end, 2000 troops were to be chasing the fugitives, not counting civilian volunteers and Indian scouts. 'Think we shall make short work of it,' Howard wired his superiors. Meanwhile, Joseph was ordering his chiefs to see that the young braves left white women and children unharmed.

On 16 June, the Nez Percé camped near the Salmon River at White Bird Canyon. They hoped to collect stock, then head westward to avoid fighting, but that was not to be. They set a trap for the troops already pursuing them, and waited.

Between 60 and 70 warriors were ready for action, about the same number having drowned their sorrows in drink to such an extent that they were unfit for action. Against them rode Captain David Perry with just over 100 men of the First Cavalry, plus 11 civilians. Even at this late hour, the Indians made a final effort to effect a truce, but one of the men in the skirmish line commanded by Lieutenant Edward Theller fired twice despite a flag of truce. The Nez Percé war had begun.

The soldiers suffered a humiliating and heavy defeat. Theller and 33 of his men were killed, the Indians suffering just three wounded. After a brief hiatus, while the Indians decided what to do next and the whites fled to towns, Howard, with almost 400 men, marched from Fort Lapwai on 22 June 1877 to be joined by yet more troops, giving him over 400. On 1 July, Howard crossed the Salmon into mountainous country, and the Indians crossed back again. The troops could not manage the crossing and it took them five days to recross at the original spot used.

On 6 July, the bands of Chiefs Looking Glass and Red Echo appeared at Joseph's camp on the south fork of the Clearwater. This brought the Nez Percé force up to approximately 150 warriors, together with some 550 women, children and older men.

At this point it must be stressed that the fighting retreat was run by leading Indians in council, with Looking Glass the most notable of the leaders. Joseph, who at White Canyon appeared to have divided his time between fighting and getting the camp with its noncombatants on the move, was the political and inspirational leader of the fugitives, as modern historians have made known. Whites never understood the fact that Indian leaders rarely had the degree of authority of white commanders, and it was naturally assumed that Joseph was indeed the military genius of the retreat. He had been dubbed the 'Red Napoleon', but until very near the end of the retreat he had no major influence on strategy. It suited white commanders, made to look so foolish by the Nez Percé, to claim that they were up against the genius of Joseph. In fact, they were facing collective genius. Joseph had the honored post of organizing the camp and the safety of the women and children.

For a short while, the fugitives rested. It was time to prepare for the march, mend equipment, and graze cattle and horses—more than 2000 animals in all. Suddenly, on 11 July, artillery fire opened up unexpectedly and a two-day battle began. It was fought with grim determination by both sides. Howard was to claim

that 23 Indians had been killed, though they later stated that only 4 had died. He did admit that 'they fought as well as any troops I ever saw.' One of his officers stated flatly that the Nez Percé were not defeated and that their retreat was 'masterly, deliberate and unmolested, leaving us with a victory barren of results.'

At a meeting on 15 July, some of whose details are obscure, it seems that Looking Glass

Below: This illustration by Frederic Remington shows the surrender of Chief Joseph of the Nez Percé to army troops. Opposite: Another version of the surrender of Chief Joseph.

suggested trying to find a home with the Crows, and, if not, with Sitting Bull in Canada. The great Sioux leader had now joined the hundreds of Sioux who had fled there in the aftermath of Custer's Last Stand. Whatever happened, the Indians started climbing the Lolo Trail the next day, en route for the buffalo ranges. The journey was a cruel one, but in 11 days they reached Montana.

In the Bitterroot Valley, they came upon a road block manned by Captain Charles Rawn, 35 soldiers, some 200 volunteers, and a band of Flathead Indians. The chiefs politely asked if they might pass and Rawn understandably refused. However, his volunteers thought otherwise, believing the Nez Percé claim that settlers would be unharmed, and the Indians went through. They passed through the Bitterroot Valley, buying provisions at a store and paying for goods that they found in an empty house. This was an Indian campaign the like of which none had experienced.

Looking Glass decided that the marchers needed a rest. This was a mistake, for Colonel Gibbon was near with 15 officers and 146 men, later to be joined by 45 volunteers. On 9 August, a dawn assault took the Nez Percé by surprise. It was a vicious attack in which women and children died, though women fought, too, alongside the men. Joseph and Looking Glass led a counterattack and Gibbon was forced to retire. The marksmanship of the Indians was noticeably better than that of the whites.

Now, with Joseph organizing the camp's retreat, a handful of warriors held off Gibbon's soldiers. Looking Glass was blamed for the decision to rest, while Nez Percé morale was shaken by the losses. And Howard was on the march again, only a day behind the Indians. He was halted by a sudden attack, then the fugitives crossed into Yellowstone Park (the first national park, created just five years before and now being enjoyed by its first visitors).

The Indians entered the park on 22 August 1877. There were still tourists in the area, two of whom were killed. Meanwhile, Looking Glass had gone ahead to sound out the Crows, hoping that they would succor the Nez Percé, but they had helped the army too often to wish to help its enemies. So the Nez Percé realized that Canada was their only hope. The Sioux had been their enemies, but surely things had changed and Sitting Bull, a refugee in Canada, would welcome them. Now, more than ever, Joseph was their inspiration.

One of several columns pursuing them was the late Colonel Custer's regiment, the Seventh Cavalry, suitably replenished after the debacle of the Little Big Horn 13 months before. The Nez Percé escaped from it after a skirmish. Howard, desparing of catching the Indians, sent an urgent message to the ambitious but efficient Colonel Nelson A Miles at Fort Keogh to march northward and cut the fugitives off.

The Nez Percé, slowed down by their sick and wounded, also pressed northward. It was fall. By the end of September, they were within 40 miles of the Canadian border. It was the time to rest a little and find some food. They did not know that Miles was near.

But his Cheyenne scouts had seen the fugitives at their Bear Paw encampment, and soon Miles was there with 600 men. A ferocious fight ensued, Miles later calling the enemy the best Indian marksmen he had ever seen. The whites lost more men than the Indians, though Toohoolhoolzote and Joseph's brother Ollokot died that day. It was another proof of the skill of the Nez Percé that their marksmen concentrated on officers and non-commissioned officers, killing seven sergeants of the Seventh. Two officers were also killed and four severely wounded.

Yet the Indians' position was now desperate. Five inches of snow had fallen, all their ponies were gone, and the only hope was that the messengers who had headed north to Sitting Bull's camp might bring him back with his braves to fight alongside them. Meanwhile, Joseph had to watch the misery of the children crying with hunger and cold, and old people suffering stoically in silence.

Miles decided to invite them to a parley. White Bird and Looking Glass refused to attend, but Joseph went. Nothing came of the talks except treachery, for Miles refused to let Joseph go. Fortunately, Lieutenant Jerome, under the impression that the Nez Percé were going to surrender, wandered into their positions and was taken prisoner, so Miles was forced to release Joseph as a trade for Jerome.

On 4 October, the fourth day of the siege, Howard arrived, much to the annoyance of Miles, who was outranked. However, he was informed that Howard would not assume command until the enemy had surrendered.

Looking Glass and White Bird still had hopes of getting help from Sitting Bull, and at a council on 5 October opposed Joseph, who wanted to reopen talks with Miles. It looked as if the Nez Percé would divide on the issue. Then, as the council ended, Looking Glass, by now determined to head northward, was hit in the forehead by a bullet that killed him instantly. That was that. 'I went to General Miles and gave myself up,' said Joseph later. Miles promised that the Indians could spend the winter at the military post on the Yellowstone, then return to Lapwai in the spring.

The story of the surrender has always belonged to Joseph because of his magnificent and heartbreaking speech, climaxed by the words: 'From where the sun now stands I will fight no more forever.' Sadly, Colonel Mark Brown, in *Montana,* January 1972, exposed the way in which Howard's aide-de-camp, Captain Charles Erskine Scott Wood, decided to improve on an already moving scene by inventing a surrender speech, when there is no actual proof that such a speech was made, or even that Joseph spoke any words at all. It is better therefore to quote what Wood wrote for the *Century Magazine* in 1884:

It was nearly sunset when Joseph came to deliver himself up. He rode from his little camp in the hollow. His hands were clasped over the pommel of his saddle, and his rifle lay across his knees; his head was bowed down. Pressing around him walked five of his warriors; their faces were upturned and earnest as they murmured to him; but he looked neither to the right nor the left, yet seemed to listen intently. So, the little group came slowly up the hill to where General Howard, with an aide-de-camp, and General Miles waited to receive the surrender. As he neared them, Joseph sat erect in the saddle, then gracefully and with dignity he swung himself down from his horse, and with an impulsive gesture threw his arm to its full length, and offered his rifle to General Howard. The latter motioned him toward General Miles, who received the token of submission.

Those present shook hands with Joseph, whose worn and anxious face lighted with a sad smile as silently he took each offered hand. Then, turning away, he walked to the tent provided for him.

Just over 400 surrendered with Joseph, less than a quarter being warriors. Ninety-eight warriors and some 200 women and children escaped across the Canadian border to Sitting Bull's camp in a pitiable condition, where they were welcomed by the Sioux and cared for. Later, some were to make the long trek home, only to find that they were regarded as troublemakers by those Nez Percé who had stayed behind.

Meanwhile, the aftermath of the poignant surrender was bitter indeed. Sherman wanted no part of Miles's promises. 'I believed Miles or I would never have surrendered,' Joseph was later to say. But, of course, those who had grabbed the Indians' lands did not want the Nez Percé back, even though, for once, the vast majority of Americans, including many Westerners, were on the Indians' side. When the captives passed through Bismarck, Dakota Territory, the townspeople cheered them, gave them food in the town square and laid on a special banquet for Joseph.

The captives were taken to Fort Leavenworth, Kansas, where more than 20 of them died of malaria that winter. After more moves in Kansas, and 47 more deaths, Joseph was allowed to visit Washington to plead for his people. They were sent to another reservation, this time in Indian Territory, where more of them died, including Joseph's baby daughter. By 1883, the scandalous treatment of the heroic Indians forced Congress to allow the Secretary of the Interior to act. So on 22 May 1885, 268 Nez Percé went back to the Northwest by train. Only 118 were allowed to go to the Lapwai reservation, the rest, including the 'dangerous' Chief Joseph, were sent to the Colville reservation in Washington.

Joseph was allowed back to his old home twice, in 1899 and in 1900. On the first visit, he tried to buy a plot of land and failed. On the second, it was made very clear to him that he would never succeed in getting what he so longed for. On 21 September 1904, he died of a broken heart, according to the agency doctor.

An old engraving of various types of Indian weapons—bow, arrows, shield, knife, and assorted forms of tomahawks.

General Sherman in council with Indians at Fort Laramie, Wyoming in 1867.

4
CONFLICT
ON THE PLAINS

In 1851, a great council was held at Fort Laramie in what was to become Wyoming. The fort, on a tributary of the North Platte, had been a famous fur-trading post. Now it saw the largest gathering of Indians ever assembled on the Plains, perhaps 10,000 of them from eight tribes, including Sioux, Cheyenne, Crow and Arapaho. Some of those present had previously met each other only on the field of battle.

In charge was an ex-mountain man, Tom Fitzpatrick, who was now an Indian agent. Everything went well. The Indians agreed not to attack each other or harass emigrants bound for Oregon or California, and even decided to let whites have and maintain roads through Indian territory. In exchange, the United States agreed to pay annual sums to the tribes and shield them from white attacks.

Three years later, the Plains Wars began.

It was not the fault of the Indians. If they had wished to, they could have wiped out the small garrison in Fort Laramie, though the post commander appeared not to recognize this. When in 1853 a Sioux took a shot at a white, he automatically assumed that the Indian was guilty and sent Second Lieutenant Hugh Fleming to arrest him. The 24-man detail failed, but got involved in a skirmish, wounding six Indians. It took much persuasion by the chiefs to keep the trouble from spreading. Said one to Fitzpatrick: 'Now the soldiers of the Great Father are the first to make the ground bloody.'

That could be described as an incident. What happened in 1854 was war—over a cow.

Fleming was now post commander. A second lieutenant had arrived fresh from West Point. His name was Grattan and he was a fool and a hothead, convinced that Indians were cowards. All he needed to crush the Sioux was a handful of infantry plus a howitzer, or so he boasted.

On 18 August, a settler went to the fort to report that an Indian had butchered one of his cows. This apparently decrepit beast had certainly been killed by a Miniconjou Sioux, who stated that it had been abandoned anyway. Grattan saw his chance for glory. When the settler demanded compensation at the fort, he urged Fleming to let him arrest the 'hostile' cow-slayer, who lived in the Brulé camp. The head chief of the Brulé, Conquering Bear, urged Fleming not to act until the government's an-

The hazards of building a railroad. Opposite above: Cheyenne attacking workers on the Union Pacific. Below: Cheyenne Indians tearing up the tracks near Russell, Kansas.

nual payments for the Indians arrived, then the money could be deducted. Grattan, however, insisted on immediate action. He got it.

He marched out the next day with 29 men and an Indian-hating French interpreter, plus a howitzer and a mountain gun. At the Brulé camp there were Indians from other subtribes of the Teton Dakotas, visiting the Brulé. The glory hunter was not deterred. He talked to Conquering Bear for half an hour while the cow killer remained in his tent, declaring he would die honorably. Finally, Grattan lost his temper and ordered his men to open fire. Conquering Bear fell, mortally wounded, while the artillery opened up. Set too high, the guns simply shredded the tops of the tepees, while the Sioux, to Grattan's surprise, instead of running away sent the soldiers fleeing with a shower of arrows. The only army survivor died in the fort a few days later.

Fortunately for the garrison, the Sioux did not attack the fort. Meanwhile, troops were rushed there and Fleming was replaced by the more experienced Major William Hoffman.

Naturally, the incident outraged the American people, and the anger was all the greater because rumor had it that the Sioux had lured the gallant Grattan to his doom. The military and the Secretary of War believed it and planned retaliation, which led to the appearance on the scene of Colonel William S Harney and 1300 men. 'By God, I'm for battle—no peace!' he was to proclaim at a time when the Indian Bureau, at least, was striving hard for peace. The situation was further complicated because five of Conquering Bear's friends had avenged him by attacking the Salt Lake stage, seizing a strongbox with $10,000 in gold in it and killing three whites while doing so.

Harney reached the Brulé camp in September, 1855 and demanded that Little Thunder, Conquering Bear's successor, hand over the killers. Little Thunder retired with his headmen under their white flag, upon which the troops advanced and opened fire. Some 85 Indians were killed and 70 women and children made prisoner.

Top: An Indian hunting buffalo, painting by George Catlin. Bottom: Sioux warrior with lance, by Frederic Remington.

Partly because they feared what might become of the women and children, the chiefs appealed to the wanted men to give themselves up. Dressed for war and singing their death songs, they surrendered at Fort Laramie, fearing the hanging that would keep them from a warrior's life in the hereafter. To the annoyance of Harney, the Indian agent prevented their execution. They were imprisoned for about a year at Fort Leavenworth, treated kindly, and then pardoned by President Pierce. One of them, Spotted Tail, was so impressed by what he had seen of white power that for the rest of his life he became a leader of the peace faction among the Sioux.

Harney himself organized the peace treaty of

1856, to the annoyance of the Indian agent, Thomas Twiss, a profiteer who resented the army spoiling his schemes. Twiss won in the end and Harney's treaty was thrown out by the Senate, but it had a fatal flaw in it. Chiefs and subchiefs were supposed to be responsible for the actions of their braves, a quite impossible condition for freedom-loving Indians. One thing was certain, however. Harney had over-awed the Sioux, and not the least reason being that they did not understand him or his men. They would learn.

Now it was the turn of the Cheyenne. They had never fought Americans, but were now to fall out with them not over a cow but over some horses. Cheyenne warriors had been raiding their old Pawnee enemies, and Harney, just before he left for another assignment, instructed the Cheyenne and their Arapaho allies to desist, otherwise he would 'sweep them from the face of the earth.'

As to the horses, there had been a dispute as to who owned them. Three were taken to the whites by the Indians, who assumed that they would be rewarded for finding the strays and looking after them, but the fourth was retained by a young brave destined to become a great fighting chief. His name was Little Wolf, and he refused to admit that the fourth horse belonged to a white man.

Tension mounted. Cheyenne who had no part in the affair were arrested, and when one was killed, others killed a white trapper. A Cheyenne camp was attacked, Indians were killed who had nothing to do with either crisis, and, inevitably, braves started attacking wagon trains.

Into the area came a rugged dragoon, Colonel Edwin V Summer, who on 29 July 1857 fought a big band of Southern Cheyenne in a battle about which Robert A Utley, a leading historian of the Indian Wars, has written that the opposing forces 'acted their parts according to the script that a later generation of motion picture and television writers would enshrine in the folklore of the West.'

Singing their war songs, 300 warriors in full battle array paraded on a hill near a lake, confident that the soldiers' bullets could not harm them because their medicine man had told them just that.

Sumner ordered a cavalry charge, a bugle blared and the cavalrymen started trotting. The colonel ordered: 'Sling—carbine. Draw—saber!' and the Cheyenne became less confident, for their medicine was protection against guns, not swords, and they broke and fled. Few were killed except those who were unhorsed and fought grimly to the end, but it was a defeat, one that made the Cheyenne realize that fighting with the whites bore little resemblance to intertribal warfare.

The peace that followed was meant to be final, but of course it was not, especially when gold was found in Colorado and thousands of whites began a rush through Cheyenne lands. Many a would-be miner was helped by the Indians. Just six years later many of those Indians were to suffer so hideously and cruelly at Sand Creek.

The Sioux and Cheyenne had been driven from the forests of Wisconsin and Minnesota in the late 18th century by Ojibwa armed with French guns. Their seven divisions and many subdivisions made up a strong alliance. The French coined 'Sioux' from the Algonquian word for enemy, their real name being Dakota, meaning allies. 'Cheyenne' may also come from 'chien', the French for dog, the Dog Soldiers being a famous Cheyenne warrior society. French traders got to know the Plains Indians in the eighteenth century before any other Europeans arrived in the area.

There were still Sioux back in Minnesota at the start of the 1860s. The 'woodland' Sioux, the Santee, though they hunted, were basically farmers, as the other Sioux had been. Now their farmlands were shrinking. By 1860, with some 150,000 whites in the area, a treaty confined the Indians to land along the Minnesota River. The treaty was not disastrous in itself, but crooked traders and officials made it so, defrauding their charges of their treaty money. Unable to afford food, unwelcome in their hunting grounds the Santee also had to endure two bad harvests in succession.

The angriest of their chiefs was Little Crow, a Christian convert who had visited Washington and had seen the President. He now lived in a house and wore white man's clothes. In 1862, he was 60 years old.

When the Civil War broke out in 1861, many

troops had been withdrawn from Minnesota. The Minnesota Sioux seemed harmless enough, but their misery should have been a danger signal. In July, 1862, after a grim winter, the Santee were due for their annual payments. Instead, they heard with dismay that their money had not yet arrived. At one agency, where thousands of Indians had gathered, Agent Galbraith was frightened enough to call in 100 soldiers. The Santee surrounded the troops and some broke into a warehouse and grabbed bags of flour. The military commander refused to fire on the Indians as he sympathized with them, and Galbraith was persuaded to issue pork and flour and be paid later. As the Santee left in a happier mood, Little Crow made Galbraith promise that he would issue supplies at the other Santee agency some 35 miles away.

Galbraith failed to keep his promise. In front of several hundred Sioux and a few settlers, Little Crow pleaded with him. Galbraith asked the traders who were in the crowd what they would do. One of them, Andrew Myrick, signed his own death warrant by replying: 'So far as I am concerned, if they are hungry, let them eat grass, or their own dung!' After an appalled silence, the Santee left.

Little Crow's situation was tragic. He had been to the East and knew the whites were numberless and could not be beaten in the end, yet his warriors understandably wanted war. Two evenings later, on 19 August, he went to church and afterward shook the hands of his white neighbors and walked away.

That night some Santee burst into his room and told him how four braves, searching for food, had killed three male and four female settlers. He rounded up the four, who wanted an uprising at once. He realized that all the Santee would be punished, but when he urged peace, he was called a coward. Stung by the taunt, he warned the braves what would happen, but agreed to lead them. It was his duty—his fate. Plans were laid and the first target chosen, the agency store.

Myrick was among the first to die, his killers filling his mouth with grass and taunting his corpse with cries of 'Now he is eating grass himself.' There followed a reign of terror for the Minnesota whites. Driven beyond endurance, the Santee killed several hundred

The battle of Beecher Island, Colorado in 1868.
Major Forsyth withstood the attacks of Sioux,
Cheyenne and Arapaho.

men, women and children with a savagery that
recalled the nightmares in the forests of the
East. Yet some went out of their way to save
those who had befriended them. Many fled to
Fort Ridgely, from which Captain Marsh and 45
men marched out, having no idea of the scale of
the uprising. They were all ambushed and only
25 got back alive. Little Crow urged his men to
take the fort, but they preferred the rich pickings at New Ulm and wasted a valuable day
when the fort could have been taken. New Ulm
could not, being strongly defended. By that
time, reinforcements had reached Fort Ridgely,
whose defenders had got their artillery in
order. There was no outer stockade, but under
Sergeant Jones the gun crews had been well
drilled on a 6-pounder, two 12-pounders, mountain artillery howitzers and some 24-pounders.
It was not that an attack had been expected.
Jones had wanted to keep his men occupied.

The first assault failed against such firepower. Ironically, along with the reinforcements came a stagecoach with the longed-for
money. The next day, fire-arrows set the roofs
of the fort alight until rain put the fires out.
Attack after attack was launched and there was
grim hand-to-hand fighting. The Santee's bravery under artillery fire was unequaled in the
whole history of the West, but they were forced
to give up, switching their attack back to New
Ulm. By now, that, too, was even better defended, and held firm.

A 1400-strong force from Fort Snelling was
now on the march, commanded by Colonel
Henry Sibley. Casualties were heavy among
them, but finally the Santee were crushed at the
Battle of Wood Lake. The uprising had lasted a
ferocious month.

The aftermath was grim. Two thousand Indian men, women and children surrendered,
392 were tried and 309 sentenced to hang—to
the joy of most Minnesotans but not the Bishop
of Minnesota, who raced to Washington to explain what had caused the uprising. Abraham
Lincoln studied the trial records and allowed
the death penalty only for proven murderers
and rapists.

A Minnesota boy who witnessed the murder of his family by the Sioux points a finger at an attacker.

On 26 December 1862, 39 Santee warriors were hanged together at the same time on a tall, specially erected gallows to the cheers of the multitude. Many more were imprisoned, while the rest, innocent as well as guilty, were driven from their lands to a worthless reservation in Dakota.

Many of the hostile Santee had escaped after the final battle and headed westward. Little Crow was one of those who got away. He vainly tried to enlist help from the Santee's cousins on the plains. He also hoped to enlist British help, as the Sioux had supported the Crown in the War of 1812, but, not surprisingly, he got nowhere when he visited Fort Garry, now Winnipeg. He and his son returned to Minnesota, aiming to steal horses and head for the plains.

On 8 July 1863, they were spotted picking berries by a deer hunter and his son. Since there was a $25 bounty on Sioux scalps, the whites opened fire, not knowing who the Indians were. Little Crow was killed, but his son escaped. The hunters scalped Little Crow, whose unidentified corpse finished up in a pit at a slaughterhouse in a nearby town. The son was captured and told what had happened. His father's killer got $500 as well as his $25 and Little Crow's son, who was only 16, was condemned to be hanged. By this time his father's body had been exhumed and his scalp and skull had become great attractions in St Paul, Minnesota. On a happier note, the son, whose name was Wowinapa, was reprieved. He lived to become the founder of the Young Men's Christian Association among his people.

Although news of the massacres in Minnesota had caused a sensation all over the plains, things remained comparatively peaceful even in Colorado, into which miners and settlers were flooding. Chastened by Sumner, the Cheyenne and their Arapaho friends were not on the warpath, though a few young braves may have joined Ute and Shoshone warriors who made things lively at times for those on the mail and emigrant routes. True, the Cheyenne fought the Ute in 1862 and 1863, but that was traditional warfare, plains style.

A crisis had broken out in 1861, when a few chiefs, among them Black Kettle of the Southern Cheyenne, signed a treaty giving away Cheyenne and Arapaho territory. In return they would get a reservation on the Arkansas River and be taught farming. In the treaty was a clause which officials were later to state allowed a railroad to cut through Indian lands, bringing white settlements in its wake.

It was the old story of whites mistaking the power of individual chiefs to speak for all, and the treaty was bitterly resented by the majority of the two tribes, who wanted freedom, not farming, beside the Arkansas. Governor John Evans of Colorado wanted both tribes there, while the Indians, apart from their obvious objections, believed that the buffalo would last for another 100 years. Why spoil a matchless life-style?

There was another white who shared Evans's feelings, an infamous man named Colonel John M Chivington.

Though a Methodist minister, he preferred soldiering, and had helped keep Confederate troops out of New Mexico. As most professional officers were fighting in the East, he was

Thirty-eight Indian warriors were hanged on a single gallows in Mankato, Minnesota after the 1862 uprising.

left in virtual control of the Denver area of Colorado. When horses began to vanish from ranches, possibly stolen by the Cheyenne, Chivington ordered troops, according to one of his officers, to 'burn villages and kill Cheyennes wherever and whenever found.'

His volunteer soldiers soon provoked the Cheyenne into fighting and the Indians found themselves at war. It was small-scale enough to have been ended by goodwill, but that was no part of Reverend Chivington's repertoire. By mid-1864, many Cheyenne were on the warpath, but not Chief Black Kettle. However, he could not restrain his wilder young men, and when the murdered bodies of a family of settlers called Hungate were displayed in Denver, many whites left their homes and made for the town, which was the territorial capital. Chivington's plans were going well. Better still, senior officers were sent to fight Confederate raiders in Missouri, leaving Chivington in charge.

Meanwhile, with the approach of fall, the Cheyenne were concentrating on hunting buffalo. Thanks to Black Kettle, white captives were returned, which displeased Evans and appalled Chivington, who needed a victory to help his political as well as his military ambi-

tions. Black Kettle was actually suing for peace. Besides, what was to become of the Third Colorado Cavalry? They had been raised from the scum of the territory as a 100-day militia, after which they would be civilians again. They needed action.

Black Kettle, imagining himself at peace, led his people to a camp south of Sand Creek, a tributary of the Arkansas. In charge there was the humane Major Wynkoop, whose removal was arranged by an officer who wanted no such humanity shown.

The Cheyenne were unaware that Evans and Chivington had arranged things cleverly enough to make it seem as if the Indians were hostiles, waiting at Sand Creek for permission from General Curtis, commander of the military Department of Kansas (which then included Colorado), to camp at Fort Lyon with the Arapaho. The fort was nearly 40 miles from Sand Creek.

All this was, of course, unknown to Black Kettle, nor did he know that Wynkoop's replacement, Major Anthony, one of Chivington's officers, was a warm admirer of his colonel.

On 28 November, Chivington and his 'Hundred Dazers' rode into Fort Lyon, to the amazement of the garrison. To keep his mission secret, he had placed guards along his line of march, ordering them to shoot anyone trying to leave. When honorable officers at the fort argued with Chivington's genocidal plans for Black Kettle's village, he cursed them and recalled old frontier sentiments: 'Kill and scalp all big and little. Nits make lice!'

Seven hundred men set out, including a few regulars and four mountain howitzers. Though Chivington later claimed that he fought 700 warriors, killing nearly 600, he actually fought 500 Cheyenne and a few Arapaho, two thirds of the total being women and children. Seeing the soldiers, Black Kettle raised both an American and a white flag over his tepee and stood beside it trying to calm his people. Chief White Antelope ran forward, urging the troops not to fire and was shot down. Escape was virtually impossible, and, though a few braves formed a line by the tepees, they were wiped out by the guns. In a small depression, some 30 warriors—with 70 women and children—formed the only real resistance.

The volunteers gleefully obeyed the order to take no prisoners, and so did the regulars. In the holocaust, women and children were hacked to pieces, ninety-eight of them being counted by one eyewitness. In all, 123 died. Chivington's troops lost 9 with 38 being wounded. The only reason that more Indians did not perish was because the ill-disciplined militiamen, many hung over from the previous night, and few of them good shots, allowed Black Kettle and many others to get away.

Chivington now went after the Arapaho, who, fortunately, had fled, so the whites headed for

Colonel John M Chivington of the United States Cavalry. He was the commander of the troops in the Sand Creek Massacre.

Denver, where scalps, arms and legs were triumphantly displayed in a theater. Some of Chivington's officers, however, were so shocked by the event that they let the truth out about the glorious victory, as did agents and traders. Congress and the army investigated and a congressional committee delivered a humane opinion. Chivington had 'deliberately planned and executed a foul and dastardly massacre which would have disgraced the veriest savage among those who were the victims of his cruelty.' Ex-mountain man Kit Carson characterized the killers as cowards and dogs. Some claimed without proof that white scalps had been found in the camp to justify 'perhaps the foulest and most unjustifiable crime in the annals of America', as Nelson A Miles, soon to be a famous Indian fighter, summed up the atrocity.

As for Chivington and his men, they could not be touched, all having left the army. As usual, the frontier belief that Indian killing was never a crime held good. The only bright spot is that when Chivington tried to enter politics, his opponents shouted 'Sand Creek' at him and he was not elected.

As usual, the settlers were the losers, for news of Sand Creek shattered the uneasy peace on the plains. The Sioux and Cheyenne Wars were about to begin.

Amazingly, Black Kettle and a few more still spoke for peace, but now the Indians turned to different leaders. Sioux, Arapaho and Cheyenne started raiding along the South Platte in January 1865. Seven Sioux and Cheyenne lured a cavalry troop from Fort Rankin farther and farther from safety, until suddenly the soldiers were confronted by scores of Indians. Eighteen of the soldiers died in the retreat to the fort. Nearby Julesburg was then ravaged, as settlers took shelter in the fort, and other settlements and stage stations were attacked. One war party came on nine ex-members of Chivington's regiment, heading east. After all nine had been killed, the Indians found Cheyenne scalps in their baggage and hacked the bodies to pieces.

Settlers, ranchers and travelers died at the hands of the Indian avengers. While Black Kettle and some Southern Cheyenne settled on a reservation with some Arapaho, having been banished forever from Colorado by a new treaty which had them sharing Kiowa land, other Cheyenne journeyed north to join their Northern Cheyenne brothers. They were near a great Sioux camp and, despite different languages and customs, they became firm allies of the Sioux.

The greatest of the Sioux at this time was the Oglala, Red Cloud, while the leading Cheyenne were Little Wolf and Morning Star, better known later as Dull Knife. Both were to achieve immortality more than a decade later.

With the end of the Civil War in April 1865, and the consequent demobilization of whole armies, there would soon be more troops in the West. Meanwhile, arguments raged in the East about the Indian question. Men of goodwill naturally hoped to turn Indians into farmers or teach them other skills. Others, though appalled by Sand Creek, wanted the destruction of the fighting tribes completed as soon as possible.

The Indians knew nothing of the debates, being more concerned in mid-1865 with the threat to their peoples and their hunting grounds. Soldiers were seen guarding roads, trails and telegraph lines, some of them north of the Platte in the undeniably Indian Powder River country.

The opening round of the campaign came in July. It happened at a bridge over the North Platte beside which was a post manned by 100 men, who were there to guard that stretch of the Oregon Trail. Though the commandant, Major Anderson, knew there were Indians in the vicinity, he had no idea that there were thousands of Indians.

Intending to burn the bridge, cross the river at a ford and then besiege the fort, the Indians vainly tried to lure some of the garrison out by using decoys. On the third day, to the Indians' amazement, a detachment of cavalry rode from the fort over the bridge and turned westward. Anderson had decided to strengthen a 25-strong escort that was bringing in five empty wagons. In command of the 25 men was Lieutenant Caspar Collins, who suddenly found himself attacked by hundreds of Sioux and Cheyenne. He ordered a retreat, but despite covering fire from troops who poured out of the fort, and howitzer shells which finally drove the Indians off, only 15 members of the detachment reached safety, all of them wounded. Collins was killed.

The wagon train was now near. In charge was Sergeant Custard, who sent four men forward when the shellfire started. Three managed to reach the fort, while Custard corralled his wagons and kept the Indians at bay. One of them, the Cheyenne, Roman Nose, was burning to avenge his brother, who had just been killed. Knowing no bullet could kill him because he was wearing his sacred warbonnet and holding a shield that was also strong medicine, he directed his braves to attack on foot. They inched their way forward, and though the soldiers kept

Above: General Philip Sheridan in conference with his officers during the Civil War. General Custer is at the far right in this photograph by Mathew Brady. Right: General George Armstrong Custer.

them out for four hours, the Indians finally overran them and burned the wagons. They rode away believing that the Powder River country would be free from whites. They then began a buffalo hunt and their annual Sun Dance.

The whites had other plans, with four columns heading toward Indian country, three led by General Connor, who had announced that Indians north of the Platte must be hunted like wolves. Hardest hit were the Arapaho, for Connor surprised and totally destroyed their camp. One of his officers noted that 'many of the female portion of this band did as brave fighting as their savage lords.'

The fourth column was led by an ex-colonel, James Sawyers. It was bound for the Montana

goldfields, and, by calling itself a road-building expedition, had been given money and a military escort. Sioux and Cheyenne under Red Cloud and Dull Knife reluctantly let the column continue in return for supplies and an agreement not to go through hunting grounds, but other Sioux later harassed the whites. The Indians kept their hold on the Powder River country, but it could only be a matter of time before the whites reappeared.

Since 1862, the pathfinder, John Bozeman, on three trips, had pioneered a route through the Powder River country to the Montana goldfields. Sawyers had used his trail. Cutting the journey to Bannack, Montana by several hundred miles, it was bound to cause conflict, and conflict on a large scale began in 1868. 'Tame' chiefs had already given the United States the right to open roads and build posts along the Bozeman Trail, though they had no authority to do so.

Custer's camp at Hidden Wood Creek during his expedition to the Black Hills of Dakota in 1874.

82

In March 1866, Chief Spotted Tail came to Fort Laramie bearing his dead daughter, having hoped to have her cured by a white doctor. The sympathetic commandant, Colonel Maynadier, gave her a military funeral and listened to the chief's recital of wrongs the Indians had suffered. Suddenly, Red Cloud appeared with his Oglala. Liking Maynadier, he said he would return when the expected peace commissioners appeared, and he agreed to sign a treaty as long as Sioux land was safeguarded. The Indians left with food, guns and ammunition.

In May, the men at the fort saw a vast council of Sioux and Cheyenne gathering nearby, including Red Cloud and 1000 braves. There were yet more Sioux to come, however, and Red Cloud demanded that the assembly should await their arrival. Disastrously, at that very moment Colonel Henry Carrington and some 700 men of the Eighteenth Infantry, plus wives and children and the regimental band, were marching toward the fort. They were under orders to build forts and outposts along the Bozeman Trail.

To avoid trouble, Carrington camped some miles from Fort Laramie, but was seen by the

Left: An Indian version of Custer's Last Stand—a pictograph made by Sioux Chief Red Horse in 1881. Above: Custer's Last Stand as the white man saw it—a lithograph by Otto Becker made in 1895. Below: As so often happens, Hollywood came up with its own version of a historical event. A poster made to advertize a 1967 film, *Custer of the West*.

m the fury and chaos of the Civil War to the glory days of the 7th Cavalry the final earth-shaking charge at Little Big Horn!

CINERAMA presents
ROBERT SHAW
USTER OF THE WEST

old in all the sweep and spectacle of CINERAMA

ARY URE
EFFREY HUNTER, TY HARDIN, KIERON MOORE, LAWRENCE TIERNEY and ROBERT RYAN

'friendly' Brulé chief, Standing Elk. He was stunned when Carrington told him the truth about his mission and he warned him what Red Cloud's reaction would be. By the time Peace Commissioner Taylor arrived, the atmosphere was electric. After one chief had spoken his mind, Red Cloud made an impassioned speech culminating in a threat to fight for his people's hunting grounds as long as he lived. Then, while an interpreter tried to translate his words over angry Indian shouts, the great chief walked away, went to his camp and ordered it to be struck.

The council collapsed as a stream of Indians hastened to join Red Cloud. Meanwhile, Carrington started out again with his overlarge force. The men had few of the new breech-loading Spencer carbines, but they did have four guns and two famous mountain men, Jim

Opposite: Custer and his Arikara Indian scouts photographed in 1873. Inset: A newspaper report of the death of Custer from the *New York World* of 6 July 1876. Left: A cavalry patrol discovers a hostile village. Below: *Attack at Dawn* by Charles Schreyvogel. Bottom: Custer attacks Black Kettle's village, 1868.

Bridger and Jim Beckworth. They were watched on the march by Indians whose presence was felt, not seen.

On 28 June, Fort Reno, built by Connor, was reached, and eight companies were left there, a quarter of Carrington's command. On 13 July, the force reached the forks of Piney Creek where Carrington decided to erect Fort Phil Kearny. On 3 August, two companies were sent to build Fort C F Smith, 70 miles from Fort Phil Kearny, which was seeing plenty of action. The Indians had begun to attack soon after Carrington had arrived. Every civilian and military wagon train was threatened, while soldiers on log detail in the 'pinery' for building the fort were continually harassed and had to be strongly guarded. Meanwhile, the Indians' strength was increasing and included the three Sioux who were to be leaders at Custer's Last Stand ten years on—Sitting Bull, Gall and a rising young warrior, Crazy Horse.

The Bozeman Trail spelled death to many that summer, one of the only parties to get through being a heavily armed cattle outfit led by Nelson Story. They were to be the last cowboys up the trail for four years.

Carrington, able enough and well-meaning, had been desk-bound in the Civil War. Now he concentrated on building rather than troop training, though two thirds of his men were recruits. His bellicose officers despised his methods, wanting action, though knowing nothing about fighting Indians. By November, with reinforcements, Carrington had 10 officers, three doctors and 389 men. Then several more officers arrived, including Captain William Fetterman, whose rashness was to lead to disaster.

Indians, including Crazy Horse, a Platte Bridge veteran, were practicing the art of decoying. Meanwhile, Carrington had been ordered to strike at the Indians in their winter camp by General Cooke, departmental commander of the Platte, who knew nothing of conditions on the Powder. The fort was nearly finished now and on 6 December there was some positive action. When the wood train was attacked yet again, Fetterman, with 30 men, dashed to its rescue.

Fetterman was a fighter but a fool. He considered Carrington a coward and despised Indians. 'Give me 80 men and I'll ride through the

Below: The Wagon Box Fight near Fort Phil Kearney, 2 August 1867. Opposite left: An Indian pipe-tomahawk. Right: An Indian fights a cavalry trooper in *The Duel* by Charles Schreyvogel.

whole Sioux Nation!' was his cry. On this occasion, he was lured down the valley, then the Indians turned, killing two cavalrymen and wounding others before Carrington arrived. The Indians, though signaling with flags and

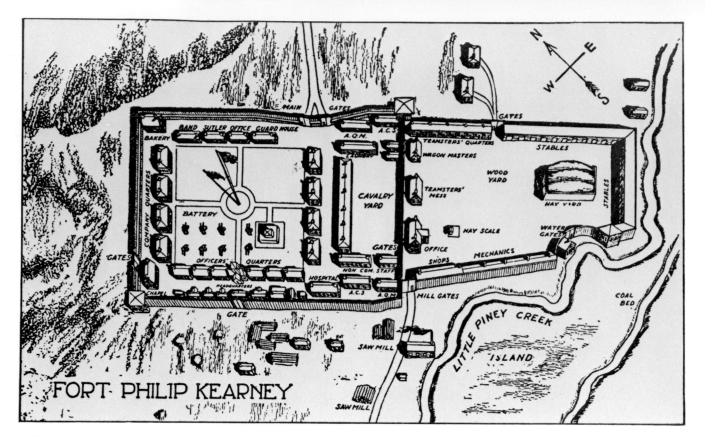

FORT·PHILIP KEARNEY

Above: An 1867 map of Fort Philip Kearney, more often called Fort Phil Kearney, on the Little Piney Creek. Note the saw mill. Right: *Defending the Stockade*—a painting by Charles Schreyvogel. Below right: The interior of Fort Laramie, painting by Alfred J Miller.

mirrors, merely frightened the raw troops and rode off to plan the next encounter.

Naturally, Fetterman failed to understand what had happened. On 19 December, the experienced Captain Powell refused to be decoyed, then on 21 December, disaster struck. With the fort almost finished, and in freezing weather, the men on the wood train set out at 10 A.M., little knowing that between 1500 and 2000 warriors were ready for them. There were ten decoys—two Cheyenne, two Arapaho, and six Sioux—the leaders being Crazy Horse, Hump, and Little Wolf. At 11 A.M., the 55-man wood detail was under attack, but the Indians had more important targets. Carrington ordered Powell to relieve the wood train, but Fetterman pleaded rank and, fatally, Carrington gave in. He ordered Fetterman simply to relieve the wood train, not go beyond Lodge Trail Ridge, and stay out of sight. Forty-nine infantrymen led by Fetterman marched out, soon followed by Lieutenant Grummond with 27 cavalrymen. Also with them were two civilians. Fetterman had his 80 men!

Carrington had a cannon fired and the decoys acted afraid, gradually moving towards Lodge Trail Ridge. They had been on foot, now they mounted and rode along the ridge, luring Fetterman's command to its doom. Moments later the sound of gunfire reached the fort.

The infantrymen died first, but the cavalrymen reached a rocky spot and died hard. It was over in less than an hour and there were no survivors. A relief force saw hundreds of Indians retreating north, then came on the victims of Fetterman's folly. The ambush had been superbly planned, and better men than Fetterman might have been lured to their doom.

The garrison prepared for an attack, not knowing that Indians rarely fought in severe winter conditions—they needed all their energy for finding food. The second night after the disaster, snow piled up against the stockade, making an assault seem even more likely. In better weather it might just have happened but, unbeknownst to filmmakers, Indians, sensibly, disliked attacking stockades.

Legend has it that John 'Portugee' Phillips rode away on the colonel's horse on the night of 21 December, to Fort Laramie, and reached there at 11 P.M. on Christmas night, a 238-mile trip (complete with brushes with the Sioux) which could have been the greatest ride in history. In fact, he and a man named Dixon both set out and both earned $300 for their undoubted bravery. Portugee was not fool enough to take only one horse, but he certainly caused a sensation at the fort and ended all Christmas revelry. Meanwhile, the Indians returned to their camps to await the spring.

General Sherman, commanding the huge Department of the Missouri, telegraphed General Grant: 'We must act with vindictive earnestness against the Sioux, even to the extermination of their women and children.' Meanwhile, Carrington was transferred, and retired in 1870, spending many years justifying his conduct, which was much criticized, unfairly perhaps; but a more experienced fighting man might have done better in very difficult circumstances.

In April of 1867, Fort Laramie had another peace council, but the Indians who mattered were not there. Railroad tracks were now heading across the West and they needed defending from the surprised, then enraged, Indians, enraged because of the slaughter of buffalo herds to feed the workers. One Cheyenne war party pulled off a classic ambush in August, 1867, first piling loose ties on the track, and lashing them down with telegraph wire. A six-man team from Plum Creek, Nebraska, hurtling along on a handpump car, crashed into the obstacle. Only one man, William Thompson, survived, and he was minus his scalp, which was too badly mauled to be sewn on again. An oncoming train went straight into the barricade and was looted by the happy Cheyenne until Pawnee scouts under Major North appeared and the laughing Indians vanished into the night. But on 10 May 1869, the continent was spanned by rail, another blow to the survival of the tribes, for troops could now be rushed to key spots.

Back in the Powder River country, the Indians in 1867 were still masters of the situation. In July, 800 warriors, mainly Northern Cheyenne, advanced on Fort C F Smith, while Red Cloud and some 1000 warriors headed for Fort Phil Kearny.

Near Fort C F Smith, 20 soldiers were guarding 12 civilian hay mowers near a wooden corral built for emergencies. It was 1 August, and the Indians, not knowing that the new Spencer repeaters and metallic cartridges had reached the troops, made little effort to surprise the whites. Only Lieutenant Sternberg was killed before the men reached the corral. The Indians tried burning the whites out, setting fire to dry grass, but the wind changed and the flames changed direction as well.

It was alleged that Colonel Brady refused to send help from the fort fearing another Fetterman incident; however, he finally sent a relief column, by which time many Indians had left. The men in the corral had survived six hours: three were killed and two were missing. A howitzer helped the Indians on their way. They may have had 100 killed or wounded.

The next day the Sioux swept down on woodcutters who were being guarded by infantrymen outside Fort Phil Kearny. Some woodcutters reached the fort, while 32 holed up in a wagon-box corral, and again it was their breechloaders that saved them. The Sioux charged valiantly again and again, but retreated finally when a relief column appeared, having lost perhaps 60 braves.

Left: A Sioux Indian village showing women working buffalo skins—painting by George Catlin. Inset: A painting of Chief Wak-tea-geli of the Dakota Indians in his full regalia.

Yet despite the soldiers' new firepower, the chances of the army winning the war were negligible. Even a massive force would prove useless against such shadowy foes, and the cost would be enormous. Though the destruction of the buffalo herds and the coming of the railroads would help the whites win in the future, the answer now seemed to be peace. Despite Sherman's demands that the Sioux should go and dwell 'forever' on a reservation along the Missouri, Red Cloud was able to refuse to surrender the Powder River country. He was in charge. In the spring of 1868, the Government gave in and agreed to abandon the hated forts. Fort C F Smith was set on fire on 30 July, the day after the troops had left, and a month later it was Fort Phil Kearny's turn. Chief Little Wolf was given the honor of setting it alight as the troops marched grimly away. In a few days, Fort Reno, too, was abandoned.

On 6 November, Red Cloud rode into Fort Laramie to sign a treaty ending a war that the Indians had won. He never again went on the warpath, though he spoke for the Indians in the West and in Washington to memorable effect. He died in 1909.

While the Northern Cheyenne were fighting in the Powder River country, their southern relatives, along with Arapaho, Comanche and Kiowa, were in a turmoil. Though many chiefs wanted peace despite Sand Creek, news of the Fetterman disaster made fighting groups like the Cheyenne Dog Soldiers want action, not loss of territory.

In Washington, there was sympathy at this time for the Indians, and not just in the Indian Bureau—a sympathy not shared by army officers and Westerners who resented the fact that authority was divided between the army and civilian agents. Naturally, the views of Westerners were the more extreme. There were conflicts about whether or not traders should sell firearms to the Indians, while officers understandably despaired when Easterners blamed the Powder River war solely on the fact that the

Indians could not get firearms with which to hunt for winter food.

Sherman meanwhile planned his next campaign. General Winfield Scott Hancock was ordered to move south of the Arkansas River and show the flag. A distinguished Civil War veteran, he had no knowledge of Indians and decided to bully the tribes on the Southern Plains. His 1867 campaign simply made a major war more certain, its most notable feat being the destruction of an empty Indian village. It was in this campaign that a young lieutenant colonel, who at 25 had been a major general of volunteers in the Civil War, fought Indians for the first time as commander of the newly raised Seventh Cavalry. His name was George Armstrong Custer.

The Medicine Lodge Treaty of 1867 which ended 'Hancock's War,' resulted in one large reservation for the Southern Cheyenne and Arapaho and another for the Kiowa, the Comanche and the Kiowa-Apache. The only whites allowed there would be teachers, agents to distribute gifts under the eyes of army officers, and men who would turn braves into farmers. The former Major Wynkoop, now an Indian agent, and a trusted friend of the Cheyenne, was with them again and the omens seemed favorable.

The first thing to go wrong was the failure of promised arms and ammunition to reach the Cheyenne. Ill-will plus misunderstandings on each side led to tension, then raids by young braves increased it. The fragile peace was over.

Major General Phil Sheridan, a fine cavalryman who believed in total war, replaced General Hancock. 'The only good Indians I ever saw were dead,' he once said, adapting the old frontier saying. He decided to attack the Indians in winter when they were short of food and their horses were weak.

Before he could implement this, an epic fight occurred at the Arikaree Fork of the Republican River in Colorado in September 1868. Major 'Sandy' Forsyth had raised a company of 50 frontiersmen to fight Indian style. They were armed with Colts and Spencer repeaters, and most were dressed as plainsmen. On the night of 17 September, 'Forsyth's Scouts' were camped by the Arikaree at a point where it was about 100 yards across. There was a narrow islet in the middle of the almost dry river with

Top: *Some American Riders,* an illustration by Frederic Remington. Below left: Rattlesnake, a Pawnee scout. Below right: Major Frank North, leader of the batallion of Pawnees.

enough grass and brush for the men to make a stand if attacked. Some braves jumped them at dawn the next day and the Scouts raced for the islet, to be surrounded by 600 or more Indians, mostly Cheyenne Dog Soldiers and Oglala Sioux.

But for the new American firepower, the first charge might have ended the fight. There were two more frontal charges that day, which also failed. Unbeknownst to Hollywood, such charges were rare.

In the afternoon the great Cheyenne chief, Roman Nose, appeared. His morale was low for his medicine was bad. He had recently eaten fried bread without realizing it had been cooked on an iron fork, and his beliefs forbade him to let metal touch his food. Before he had finished purification rites, he had to rush to help his people, though he knew he was doomed. In his splendid warbonnet, he led his men against the whites, but even the Southern Cheyenne could not survive the hail of bullets that met them. Roman Nose, once invincible, was mortally wounded in the spine.

Forsyth survived three bullets that desperate day. Lieutenant Beecher, whose name was given to the islet, was killed, and half the other scouts were dead or dying. But two men escaped and reached Fort Wallace. On 25 September, Captain Carpenter and men of the 10th Cavalry rescued the remnants of Forsyth's command. He had had 6 killed and 15 wounded, but the Indians had lost some 40, though the whites were to claim far more. Desolated at the loss of Roman Nose, the survivors rode to join Black Kettle, the peace lover, who, like Roman Nose, was also doomed.

Custer was to be the instrument of Black Kettle's doom, Custer the glory hunter, the possessor of Custer's luck. He did not hate Indians. He was too like them himself. He and the Sioux understood each other. He and they wanted glory and he would fight them because he liked action, fame and promotion. Ambitious and boastful though he may have been, he surely stated the truth when he wrote that if he were an Indian, he would greatly prefer to 'cast my lot among those of my people who adhered to the free open plains, rather than submit to the quiet, unexciting uneventful life of a reservation.' As for his luck, despite being courtmar-

Far left: An Indian scalper. After killing his victim, the warrior cut the skin from his head and saved it as a trophy. Below: Plainsmen holding off Indians in *A Check—Keep Your Distance*, a lithograph by Currier and Ives, 1853. Left: The Indians depended on the buffalo for food and for skins to make clothing from. In this painting by George Catlin, Sioux hunters are chasing a herd of those animals.

tialed and suspended for a year for a mammoth list of crimes, he was recalled at the urgent request of Sheridan for a winter campaign in 1868.

Meanwhile, Black Kettle was still preaching peace, knowing it was his people's only hope. His position was weakened as he did not have his young warriors under control, admitting as much to General Haven, in command of Fort Cobb, Indian Territory. Sheridan had already declared war on all hostiles, meaning any Indians who happened to be Southern Cheyenne, and Haven could only urge the chief to deal directly with Sheridan and try to control his young men. Saddened, Black Kettle returned to his camp beside the Washita River in Indian Territory.

It was late November, and Custer, with 800 men, was heading there. Wet snow was on the ground as he neared the village on the night of 26 November. He split his men into four groups to surround it for a dawn attack. The cold in-

creased and the river was covered with ice.

There were four white captives in the camp, but Black Kettle believed he could surely return them to the whites, who might then leave the Indians in peace. He never got his chance to parley. At dawn, buglers of the Seventh Cavalry sounded the charge, and the band struck up the regimental march *Garryowen*—until their instruments froze. Black Kettle and his wife died early in the battle. The Cheyenne tried to flee but were surrounded, so they prepared to die bravely, some women fighting with the men, other women desperately trying to escape with their children.

Nearby Arapaho arrived to help their friends, cutting off a detachment led by Major Elliott, which was pursuing women and children. With the fight almost over, Kiowa and Comanche suddenly appeared on a hill above the camp. While some troops held them off, the rest destroyed the village and nearly all the Cheyenne's pony herd, an even worse blow than the destruction of food and tepees. The regiment advanced on the other Indian camps, forcing the Cheyenne's allies to hasten home. The move was a bluff. Custer suddenly wheeled from the valley and started back to his base at Camp Supply, where Sheridan rejoiced at the fate of the savages, Black Kettle included, who, he claimed, had been offered sanctuary and refused it. Others reacted differently. Agent Wynkoop stated publicly before resigning that Black Kettle had been betrayed.

Some claimed that the Washita was another Sand Creek. It was not. There were hostiles in the camp and white captives, and many women died fighting. Yet the battle brought no credit on the army, for most Cheyenne wanted peace. Instead, nearly 100 women and children had been killed and 53 taken prisoner. The Seventh claimed 103 dead warriors, the Cheyenne said only 13 had died. As for Custer, his reputation with many of the Seventh's officers was badly damaged because they felt he had failed to search for Elliott and his 19 men. The regiment's morale was never the same again.

Now the Cheyenne split on the question of war or peace, Little Robe following Black Kettle's example, the Dog Soldiers heading north to join the Northern Cheyenne. On the way, many were killed in an attack by Major North and his Pawnee scouts. It was the end of the Southern Cheyenne as a warrior race.

In 1870, two years after Red Cloud's War had ended in triumph, a Wyoming newspaper proclaimed that the same 'inscrutable arbiter that decreed the downfall of Rome, has pronounced the doom of extinction upon the Red Men of America.' Friends of the Indians were less likely to blame the arbiter and more likely to point to white greed. Certainly it was greed for gold that triggered off the most famous Indian war of all, the war which culminated in Custer's Last Stand.

Although Red Cloud, Spotted Tail and other chiefs had given up actual fighting, they did their best with words to prevent white invasions of Indian land and to stop forced tribal migrations to sites chosen by whites. In the East at least, they often received a sympathetic hearing. Other Plains Indians continued their old life that was so soon to vanish, a life of hunting the buffalo and raiding old tribal enemies.

One Indian above all others was emerging among the Sioux, a leader who wanted no truck at all with the whites and their promises. He was Sitting Bull, and he gradually became not only the most influential Hunkpapa Sioux but the dominating figure among all the Sioux tribes, even of the Northern Cheyenne and the Arapaho. There were other heroic figures—Crazy Horse, Rain-in-the-Face and the Cheyenne Two Moon were just three of them—but none equaled the great warrior, religious leader and politician that was Sitting Bull.

The heartland of the Sioux, though once it had been Cheyenne territory, was the Black Hills. The Sioux had found gold there, but they had been advised by the missionary Father de Smet and by friendly traders, to keep their finds secret. A few whites penetrated the hills, but though they found signs of gold, at first they were kept out by the military.

The crucial year was 1874. To the delight of the whites, an expedition commanded by Custer was sent to the hills. He had 1000 men, including ten troops of the Seventh Cavalry, two companies of infantry, 60 Indian scouts, army engineers, scientists, newspapermen, two miners and a photographer, plus three Gatling guns. Custer was ordered to find a suitable spot for a military post, but the presence of miners gave away the other purpose of the expedition. And gold was found, enough for the news to ring round the nation. By Christmas, the first prospectors were on the 'Thieves' Road', as the Sioux called Custer's route. The army tried and failed to keep them out, and by mid-1875, 1000 or so illegal miners were there, with more on the way.

The government decided to try to buy the hills, sending a commission, protected by cavalrymen, west. Stormy meetings took place. Six million dollars was offered, but Red Cloud demanded 70 million and insisted that the government support the Sioux for 200 years.

Many Sioux wanted no part in the selling. Crazy Horse summed up their feelings, saying: 'One does not sell the earth on which the people walk.' There were angry scenes, which showed the commissioners the depth of Indian feeling, then the whites left, glad to have kept their scalps. Crazy Horse and Sitting Bull had refused to attend the conference.

The number of whites in the sacred Black Hills was growing every day, so an order went out that all Sioux must be on the reservations by the end of January 1876, or be considered hostile. It mattered not at all that many Indians had never signed the 1868 treaty. Sitting Bull had no wish to fight and had no prejudice against whites, but, like other Sioux leaders, was ready to fight for the Black Hills—31 January meant nothing to such men.

'Unless they are caught before early spring they cannot be caught at all,' said Sheridan, but the winter was too cold to allow a campaign. In the north, General Terry hoped to send Custer out, but snows halted supplies. However, General Crook, whose headquarters was at Omaha, Nebraska, managed to assemble 900 men at Fort Fetterman, Wyoming, in late February. They were ordered up the Bozeman Trail.

Despite the appalling weather, Crook, recently a successful commander against the Apache, pushed on and approached a Sioux and Cheyenne campsite near the mouth of the Little Powder River. Among the Sioux was Crazy Horse's friend, He Dog, who, like many Indians, had decided to go to the agency but only when the snows melted. Many had missed the deadline for the same reason, and if they had reached it they would probably have starved. Food was so short there that in March many of those who had gone to the agency simply left.

On 17 March, a young brave spotted Crook's advance column, which was led by Colonel Reynolds. It was dawn, and the troops thought that they had surprised Crazy Horse's camp. They swept through the village in three columns. The Indians rallied, steered their families to safety, surrounded their village and began firing down on the soldiers who were burning the tepees.

The whites were forced to retreat, while the Indians recaptured half their horses from them. Though their village was destroyed, there was only one Indian casualty. Four whites had died and over 60 were suffering agonies from frostbite.

Crook was furious and brought charges against Reynolds, but Sherman realized that the weather was the decisive factor and canceled the campaign until the summer.

In April 1876, there was a great council of Sioux, Cheyenne and Arapaho in the valley of the Tongue River. 'We are an island of Indians in a lake of whites,' said an angry Sitting Bull. 'We must stand together or we will be wiped out one by one. The soldiers want war. We will give it them.' The words were carried by runners to camps and the agencies, and, despite Red Cloud's warnings, many 'tame' Indians, including his own son, Jack Red Cloud, left for Sitting Bull's camp to join in the war that Red Cloud knew would end in final disaster.

The whites planned a three-pronged attack. From the east, Terry and Custer were advancing with some 925 men. There were 700 in the Seventh Cavalry, three companies of infantry, 40 Arikara scouts and a detachment in charge of three Gatlings. This impressive force left Fort Abraham Lincoln, Dakota Territory, on 17 May. Meanwhile, 450 men under Colonel John Gibbon were heading eastward, and Crook with 1000 men was heading up the Bozeman. Gibbon was under orders to cut off the Indians driven north by Crook.

In June, Sitting Bull and the Hunkpapa held their annual Sun Dance in the huge camp housing Sioux, Cheyenne and Arapaho. This was the supreme moment of Sitting Bull's career. With none of the real power to influence American history that his mighty predecessors, Pontiac, Brant, Tecumseh and a few more, had possessed, he embodied all their aspirations. As a medicine man as well as a warrior, he decided to be one of those who looked for a vision in the sacred ceremony. He offered a hundred pieces of skin from his arms, and a Sioux

Below: A photograph of an Arapaho family taken in the 1890s. Inset: Typical moccasins of the Plains Indians. Above: A photograph of the famous chief of the Shoshoni Indian tribe, Washakie. Chief Washakie was born in 1804 and died in 1900.

Above, three Cheyenne, possibly (left to right) White Antelope, Man on a Cloud and Roman Nose, photographed in 1868. Left: Two Cheyenne, Chief Dull Knife (seated) and Little Wolf. Photographed by W H Jackson, about 1877.

named Jumping Bull said he would serve him. While Sitting Bull sat leaning against the central pole in the Sun Dance circle, his server, using a steel pricker and a sharp knife, cut out the pieces of skin until Sitting Bull's arms were a mass of blood. The chief sat motionless chanting to Wakan Tanka, the Great Spirit, as the Indians watched his half-hour ordeal.

Then came the dancing; it went on all day and all night and into the next morning, until noon found Sitting Bull exhausted. He was laid on the ground and water was thrown in his face, which brought him back from a faint. He told Black Moon about the vision he had seen and Black Moon told the assembled throng how Sitting Bull had heard a voice from on high saying: 'I give you these because they have no ears.' At this Sitting Bull had looked up and seen soldiers coming down like grasshoppers, with their heads down and their hats falling off.

They were falling into the Sioux camp.

None doubted the vision's meaning. The unheeding whites, ready to fight an unjust war, were on their way and, as they were upside down, it signified that they would die. Victory would be to the Sioux. It was 14 June, eleven days before Custer and his men would be wiped out.

The tribes moved to a camp beside a stream flowing into the Little Bighorn River. There may have been some 15,000 in all, 4,000 of them warriors. There were five Sioux tribal circles there and one Cheyenne circle, and with the Cheyenne were some Arapaho friends.

Crook's column was the first in action. On 16 June, it reached the Rosebud, a tributary of the Yellowstone. The next morning, 1000 or so Indians struck when the troops were having a coffee break. Crook, Shoshone, and Crow scouts held them at bay for the 20 vital minutes, then the full fury of a determined enemy struck the whites. The battle swung against the Indians as Crook's men cleared the heights above them, but Crook, believing wrongly that Crazy Horse's village lay north, sent a squadron to attack it, then began to pull the rest of his command out of the fight to follow the squadron. This led to the whites being assailed from three directions.

This was Crazy Horse's day. When the whites charged, instead of hurling them into the rifle fire, Crazy Horse had the Indians break away to either flank, and penetrate the weak spots in their lines, which soon became impossible to hold firm. As the troops tried to survive in small groups, the braves darted backwards and forwards. Some of the soldiers would follow, and be isolated and killed.

The most celebrated moment in the fight came when Cheyenne Chief Comes-in-Sight had his horse shot from under him when leading a charge. His death seemed certain when, suddenly, a horse and rider raced to cover his body from the rifle fire. Seconds later, he leaped up behind the rider, who raced to safety. The rider was his sister, Buffalo-Calf-Road-Woman, who had seen him fall when she was helping with the horse herd. The Cheyenne called the Battle of the Rosebud 'The Battle Where the Girl Saved Her Brother.'

It was a six-hour fight, with the Indians at last forgetting that war was a great game and fighting for their lives and liberty instead. Finally, Crook was rescued by the troops he had sent forward. He was an inspired fighter against the Apache, but this was not his day, though he dared to claim a victory because the triumphant enemy rode away. He had been beaten, and he retreated as fast as he could with his wounded, and then refused to move until reinforced. And thus he missed the climax of the campaign.

The grass was good, and so was the hunting, in and around the great Indian camp. There was a victory to celebrate, there were dances and meetings of the chiefs. Meanwhile, Terry, knowing nothing of Crook's failure, had held a conference aboard the Far West, a steamboat on the Yellowstone River. General Gibbon had just reached him, and it was decided to send the Seventh's second-in-command, Major Marcus Reno, to reconnoiter. He was looking at empty Indian campsites, unaware that Crook was in action elsewhere. Reno went farther south than he should have done and spotted signs of a great Indian trail. Terry upbraided him for his pains, fearing that he might have been seen. The general feared that the Indians might escape as they had done before. He ordered Custer up the Rosebud and down the Little Bighorn from the south, Crow scouts having spotted smoke in that direction. Gibbon was to cross the Yellowstone by ferry, march up the Bighorn into the Little Bighorn Valley, descending from the north. It was assumed that Custer would fight a battle and that Gibbon could cut off fugitives.

Terry's exact orders have been argued over ever since, especially because of the amount of leeway that Custer was permitted if anything unexpected occurred. Yet what none of the white leaders could have known was the sheer size of the Indian force and its determination and the tactical brilliance of its leaders.

Custer marched away on 22 June with more than 600 men, plus six extra scouts, all of them Crows. They knew the area better than his Arikara scouts. He decided against taking Gatling guns, thinking that they might slow him down.

The regiment's morale was not high. The divisions caused by the Washita were still there, and Custer himself was lucky to be present. Having dared to attack fort traders and their corrupt bosses, and spoken out in Washington on the subject, he had fallen afoul of President Grant, whose brother was one of those accused. Forbidden to return to the West, Custer was finally allowed back because of his reputation as an Indian fighter. He badly wanted a victory, but it was observed that his spirits were lower than usual on the march. On 23 June, he forced the pace, passing deserted campsites and little knowing that he was in a huge circle of camps. His scouts were just beginning to realize what they were up against, but not Custer.

The Indians knew on the 24th that soldiers were near, though they did not know which soldiers. While Custer was telling his Arikara that one day he would be the Great White Father in Washington, Sitting Bull was praying on a hilltop for victory. And that night Custer followed the Indian trail instead of heading up the Rosebud. If he had won, none would have dared criticize him. He told his officers that, having followed the trail to the divide between the Little Bighorn and the Rosebud, they would rest on the 25th. The attack would follow on the 26th, by which time Gibbon and his men would be in position.

After an exhausting night march, the scouts spotted the Indian villages some 12 miles away. Fearing that the hostiles might retreat before he could engage, Custer, given the size of the encampment ahead, fatally divided his command. Captain Benteen was sent south with 125 men to search for hostiles, Major Reno was ordered straight ahead with 112 men to attack the southern end of the camp, while one troop was ordered to escort the pack train in the rear. Custer, with 215 men, prepared to advance on Ash Creek, which is now Reno Creek.

Custer and Reno, starting together, saw dust ahead caused by some Sioux who seemed to be running away, though in fact they were the rear guard of one of the camps moving to the main village. Reno was ordered to attack and told that 'the whole outfit would support him.'

In the huge Indian gathering, hunting parties were coming and going, women were digging up wild turnips and boys were swimming in the Little Bighorn. Many of the Indians had firearms, some even having Winchesters, including

Opposite: Chief Sitting Bull of the Hunkpapa Sioux. Inset: Chief Two Moon of the Cheyenne. He fought at the Little Big Horn.

Sitting Bull, who had two revolvers as well. Others had bows and war clubs. And Custer had no Gatlings. A dust cloud heralded the arrival of the Seventh, and there was a rush for the camp by women and children as Reno's men appeared, spread out in line and charged, firing their carbines.

Seizing their weapons, the Sioux mounted their horses and opened fire, covering their families' retreat. The attack so startled some of the horses that their would-be riders had to fight on foot.

The gunsmoke was seen at the Cheyenne camp some four miles away. A Sioux raced up to the Cheyenne chief Two Moon, calling: 'Soldiers come! Plenty white soldiers!' and the Cheyenne prepared for action. As Two Moon galloped to the fight, he saw the Sioux starting to drive the whites back until gunsmoke and dust hit them.

Gall, Sitting Bull's 26-year-old adopted brother, led the fight to turn Reno's men back. The soldiers were dismounted now, firing on foot for accuracy; but they were forced to retreat, first to a cottonwood grove, then, having mounted again, across the river on to the small hills beside it.

'Be brave, boys. It will be a hard time,' called Sitting Bull, who was surprised so few whites had charged. He rightly guessed that the Bluecoats had assumed that they would be supported. Custer had other plans.

Heading north along the line of the river, but hidden by cliffs, he had ridden to the top for a moment, seen the encampment, then the start of Reno's charge. Waving his hat at them, he sent a message to Benteen ordering ammunition. Trumpeter Martini, the messenger, was the last white man to see Custer and his 215 men alive. No one knew or knows just what happened to them in the confused fighting that followed, for there was a pall of gunsmoke over the battlefield, but the basic facts are reasonably clear.

Half Reno's command had been lost when the hostiles suddenly started to melt away. They had heard that more soldiers were riding

toward their camp and, with Reno pinned down, Gall sent some of his warriors to combat the new threat. The Indians headed across the Little Bighorn, then through a gap in the bluffs and rode into action 'like a hurricane', as one old brave later recalled. Custer's men fell back to a high ridge, only to be attacked by warriors of Crazy Horse and Two Moon on their flanks and rear. The whites must have known now that they were doomed.

They dismounted and made their final stands, broken up into smaller and smaller groups until there were none left alive. Many Indians later recalled their enemies' bravery with admiration. Contrary to legend, not until near the end of the fight did some of the Indians realize who had attacked them. Custer had had his long hair shorn, and though several warriors were

Above: Chief Rain-in-the-Face of the Hunkpapa Sioux tribe. Below: Sioux Chief Sleeping Bull with cavalry saber, 1877.

later to claim that they had killed him, nothing was ever proved to be certain. Possibly several did, as an Arapaho stated. He had seen Cheyenne closing in on a badly wounded man in buckskins. Two brothers of Custer and a nephew also died in the holocaust, a ferocious fight that lasted less than an hour.

Benteen and his men, advancing after Custer's order, found themselves amid the remnants of Reno's command. All could hear heavy firing and Reno had to forbid some of his officers from heading toward it. Some started anyway, only to be driven back. Reno was to be made the scapegoat for the disaster, but he could never have saved Custer. Meanwhile, the pack train had reached Reno and the men dug themselves in. Attacks went on all day and started again the next morning when the Indians suddenly rode away. They had heard that more white troops were arriving and, though they had failed to take Reno's strongly defended position, they had already won a great victory. Only Comanche, Captain Keogh's horse, was left alive on the Custer battlefield, and in all 260 whites were dead or mortally wounded. It was the greatest defeat inflicted on whites by Indians in the whole of the 19th century. Sitting Bull's vision had been a true one.

News of the battle reached the American people on 5 and 6 July, just after the United States had been celebrating its 100th birthday. Rage was mixed with humiliation and a fierce desire for revenge. First to suffer were Indians who had remained at peace. Reservation Sioux became virtual prisoners of war and the government swiftly passed a law to annex the Black Hills and the Powder River country. Also the Sioux were to be forced onto a new reservation beside the Missouri. Red Cloud summed up the chiefs' despair when he said: 'I think if my people should move there they will all be destroyed. There are a great many bad men there and bad whisky.'

Troops poured into the West by rail. Winter was coming and, with the buffalo herds dwindling fast, the victorious Indians were destined to be desperately short of food. Their hour of triumph was the prelude to their doom.

General Crook, who heard about the battle only three weeks later, prepared for action, but the Indians had split up and were hunting. He joined up with Terry, who was after Sitting Bull. Colonel Nelson A Miles, a rising star, was ordered to hold the Yellowstone Valley that winter and Crook himself headed into the Black Hills, a grim march because of lack of food and appalling weather. Not an Indian was seen until the camp of the Sioux American Horse was struck. The chief was mortally wounded and the Indians surrendered. Suddenly, Crazy Horse swept down on the Americans at the head of 200 warriors, but was outnumbered and retreated. It was the only American victory in 1876.

Meanwhile, Miles, offering a reservation or a fight, caught up with Sitting Bull, a meeting that went badly and ended in a two-day running battle. In the end, Miles, an able commander who had artillery, forced the Indians to retreat. Sitting Bull with some of his braves escaped to Canada in May 1877, where many Sioux had already fled.

Crazy Horse was still at large. Crook was after him with 11 troops of cavalry, 15 of infantry, plus artillery, a supply train of 168 wagons and a 400-mule pack train—2000 men in all, including 400 Indian scouts. They were heading for the Rosebud battlefield, where Crook believed Crazy Horse to be, when news arrived of a Cheyenne village in the Bighorn Mountains. Colonel Ranald Mackenzie was sent with 1000 men to attack it.

It was the camp of Dull Knife and Little Wolf, and, though the Indians got their wives and children to safety before opening fire on the whites, they were forced to retreat when the soldiers destroyed their village. After a grim winter march they reached Crazy Horse's village and, with too little food and ammunition, the Indians' joint situation became desperate.

Crazy Horse moved to a new camp on the Tongue River. Since some of his warriors wanted to give in, he allowed a party of braves under a flag of truce to go to Fort Keogh, where Colonel Miles was stationed. These men were set upon by Miles's Crow scouts. In a rage, Miles had the scouts dismount and sent their horses to Crazy Horse, but the chief had led his people away.

Sporadic fighting continued, but finally even Crazy Horse had had enough. Red Cloud and Spotted Tail (he was related to both) urged him to come in, and he did so after being promised a reservation in the Powder River country. Leading 1000 men, women and children, he marched into Camp Robinson, Nebraska, on 6 May 1877 and threw his three Winchesters on the ground in front of Crook. It seemed that the Sioux Wars were finally over. There were a few hostiles at large who would soon be cornered by Miles, but the glory days were over.

Or were they? Crazy Horse was worshiped by the young warriors, which annoyed the older ones and the whites. No news of his reservation came through and he refused to go to Washington with a delegation as others had done and were doing. The wars might be over but his soul remained free. Some Sioux went to help crush the Nez Percé, but, for all the cult of freedom allowed to individual Indians, this defection was impossible for Crazy Horse to understand. And surely those Sioux scouts might be used to track down Sitting Bull!

What happened next was tragic and remains controversial. Crazy Horse's feelings were well enough known for army reinforcements to be drafted in case of a breakout. Before Crook left to fight the Nez Percé, he ordered the chief's arrest. Crazy Horse set out for Spotted Tail's camp, perhaps hoping to raise a new band, but soldiers caught up with him and brought him back to the fort on 5 September 1877. Told he was to see Crook, he was then informed that it was too late and was put in the charge of a white officer and an Indian policeman, one of his own warriors and a friend, Little Big Man.

He was led to a guardhouse, and in the doorway tried to break away. He drew a hidden knife, but Little Big Man grabbed his arms. Some Indians, who had once been his friends, shouted: 'Shoot! Shoot to kill!' but it was a white guard who gave him a mortal stab wound with his bayonet. It is reported that Crazy Horse gasped: 'Let me go, my friends. You have hurt me enough.' He died that night aged 35.

Those Indians who had feared him because he might have upset the peace, now mourned him. His true friends' hearts were broken.

With Crazy Horse out of the way, the whites could plan the move to the Missouri. Most of the Indians would finally be in Dakota Territory, where the last tragedy would be played out.

And now it was the turn of the Northern Cheyenne to achieve immortality. Shortly before Crazy Horse's death, they had reached a wretched reservation in Indian Territory. Another promise—of a home in the north—had been broken, despite the fact that some of the warriors had acted as scouts under a sympathetic officer, Lieutenant Clark. Crook promised that they could return if they did not like their new home.

Nine hundred thirty-seven Cheyenne reached it in mid-1877 and a terrible period began. With few of their possessions, they were faced with more prosperous Southern Cheyenne, who were not always friendly, and also a well-meaning agent who meant to make them farmers. Far more serious was the unhealthy climate for Indians used to the high country of Montana, while most local game had been exterminated. Fever was rife and there was no hope of going home. Their agent, Miles, and their military commander, Lieutenant Lawson, tried to get them beef, but it was of poor quality. After a year, 50 children had died of the dread 'coughing sickness,' and other diseases returned in the hot weather.

When Miles still could not promise a return north, Dull Knife and Little Wolf decided it was time to escape. Miles was actually warned by the Indians of what they intended to do, but could not believe it. They had seen the new railroads and the telegraph wires that could summon up troops. They had seen the settlers swarming into the West now that the myth of the 'Great American Desert' had been exploded. Yet on 9 September 1878, they set off—284 Cheyenne, only 87 of them warriors. They were short of rifles, but they were going home.

Cavalry from Fort Reno and Camp Supply, both in Indian Territory, caught up with them on their fourth day out. An Arapaho scout was sent to parley. He was told that the Cheyenne were going home and would not attack unless attacked first. Little Wolf rode after the Arapaho hoping to reason with the soldiers, but a volley was fired and a battle began. It was

Above: The Sun Dance Ritual of the Sioux Indians. Left: A woman of the Sioux working on a hide. Photo from the 1870s. Center: Chief American Horse in a shirt trimmed with scalps. Right: Chief Red Cloud of the Oglala Sioux.

waged again the next day until the soldiers gave up. The Cheyenne were never overtaken again.

Crossing Kansas, they fought a succession of running battles with troops, cowboys and settlers. Little Wolf tried to stop his young braves from settling old scores, but there was one deliberate attack on a settlement where Cheyenne had been slaughtered some years earlier. They crossed the Nebraska line, joining up again after moving in small groups for safety. Now Dull Knife wanted to stop. 'This is our country. Nothing evil has ever happened to us here.' Lit-

tle Wolf disagreed and said that he and his band would head north. So that night Dull Knife left with 45 warriors, 61 women and 42 children, and in the morning Little Wolf started out with 40 warriors, 43 women and 38 children.

In late October, with snow falling, Dull Knife's band, bound for Red Cloud or Spotted Tail's camp, was surrounded by cavalry. They were told that the Sioux leaders had been taken north, but that the Cheyenne could come to nearby Camp Robinson. Reluctantly they agreed, but wisely disassembled their best weapons and hid them, the women putting bar-

Above: Red Shirt of the Oglala Sioux. Above left: Slow Bull (left), an Oglala. Center left: Crazy Horse, chief of the Sioux, from a painting by Robert Lindneux. Bottom left: Mahpiya Iuta, or Scarlet Cloud, also known as Red Cloud, 1900.

rels under their clothes and tying mechanical parts to moccasins and beads to make them seem to be ornaments. Old weapons were displayed to be handed over if necessary, and the next morning the order came and the weapons were piled on the snow, bows included. They were allowed to keep only their knives.

They were placed in a hut at the fort. At least they were out of the cold and they hid their weapons under the floorboards. The soldiers were friendly enough, but there was no news of a transfer to Red Cloud's camp. The commandant needed orders first, but at least some braves were allowed to hunt.

A new commandant, Captain Wessels, arrived, who was deeply suspicious of the Cheyenne. Red Cloud visited them and spoke up for them but warned against disobeying the white man. Then Dull Knife publicly addressed Wessels, stating flatly that his people would kill each other rather than go south again.

On 3 January 1879 they were ordered south—at once—through winter blizzards. Dull Knife refused to move, and after five days during which they refused to change their minds, the Indians were imprisoned in their hut—food, fuel and water supplies being cut off. On the 9th, after another confrontation in which a guard was stabbed, Wessels demanded that the women and children be let out to prevent further suffering. The Cheyenne replied that they would all die rather than go south, so, fearing a breakout, troops placed iron bars on the hut's doors and six guards patrolled outside.

Inside, the Indians were reassembling their weapons and turning flooring and stoves into weapons. They painted their faces, embraced each other and waited to die. Fortunately, Wessels believed a breakout was impossible, but it began around 10 o'clock that night. One hundred thirty Cheyenne were poised to escape, 44 of them men and boys. Little Shield raised his rifle and shot the sentry outside one window and, seconds later, the Cheyenne erupted from the other windows, firing as they came. Rifles were grabbed from dead and dying soldiers.

Men began pouring out of their barrack rooms, some still in their underwear, by which time the Dog Soldiers were well placed outside the fort on raised ground, covering the retreat of the women and children: there was no stockade round the fort. The Cheyenne could have escaped by now if all had been warriors, but they would not abandon any women or children.

Casualties among the escapers became heavier as they raced for a bridge over the White River. Those carrying saddles and equipment now threw them away, for there was no chance of seizing horses. Only in the hills beyond the reach of cavalry could they hope to survive. Wounded warriors lay in the snow singing their death songs, some being finished off by the soldiers, others being taken back to the fort to have their wounds dressed.

Now the fugitives reached the river, drinking greedily after several days without water. Then they were attacked. Women and boys seized rifles from the dead and began firing, and some of their enemies were now so frozen that they had to return to the fort. Cavalry replaced them. Over 50 prisoners were brought back in the morning, many badly wounded. Wessels asked: 'Now will you go south?', and a woman shouted: 'You have killed most of us. Why not finish your work?'

But the fight still raged, with fewer warriors using more rifles. Day after day it continued, with some whites behaving like butchers, others showing kindness, especially to children. (Even Wessels saved one child.)

Amazingly, the fight, which had begun on 9 January, continued until the 21st, and its final moments were among the grandest in the whole tragic history of the Indian Wars. Thirty-five men, women and children were in a hollow some 35 miles from the fort, having endured attacks by infantry, cavalry and artillery. With hardly any ammunition left, they sang their death songs and waited for the end. The soldiers poured bullets into the hollow for three hours, then charged. The charge failed. Yet the Indians were being shot one by one as they had to leap up over their rough parapets to see their targets. The whites demanded their surrender time and again until the Indians' ammunition ran out and troopers rushed to the edge of the pit, shooting, then falling back. There could be none left alive now.

Suddenly, three braves, drenched in blood, rose from the pit and began to charge. They were the last men left alive. One had an empty pistol, the others knives. They charged the 200 and fell, riddled with bullets.

Twenty-three dead were lifted from the pit. There were only two Indians that were not wounded, both women. Dull Knife and some of his family had got away to the Pine Ridge Reservation. Would the wounded and the captives back at Camp Robinson now be forced back to Indian Territory?

As it happened, news of the Cheyenne's heroism had so stirred public opinion that they were allowed to settle with the Sioux. Finally, they were returned to Montana, which Little Wolf and his band had reached in safety. They had hidden through the winter in Nebraska, then started north to be found by their friend, Lieutenant Clark, who told them how things had changed. Many became valued scouts: the army had always admired the valor of the fighting Cheyenne. The years following their epic flight were difficult for the Northern Cheyenne, but at least they were years spent in their beloved homeland.

Geronimo and three of his Chiricahua warriors at the time of his conference with General Crook in March 1886.

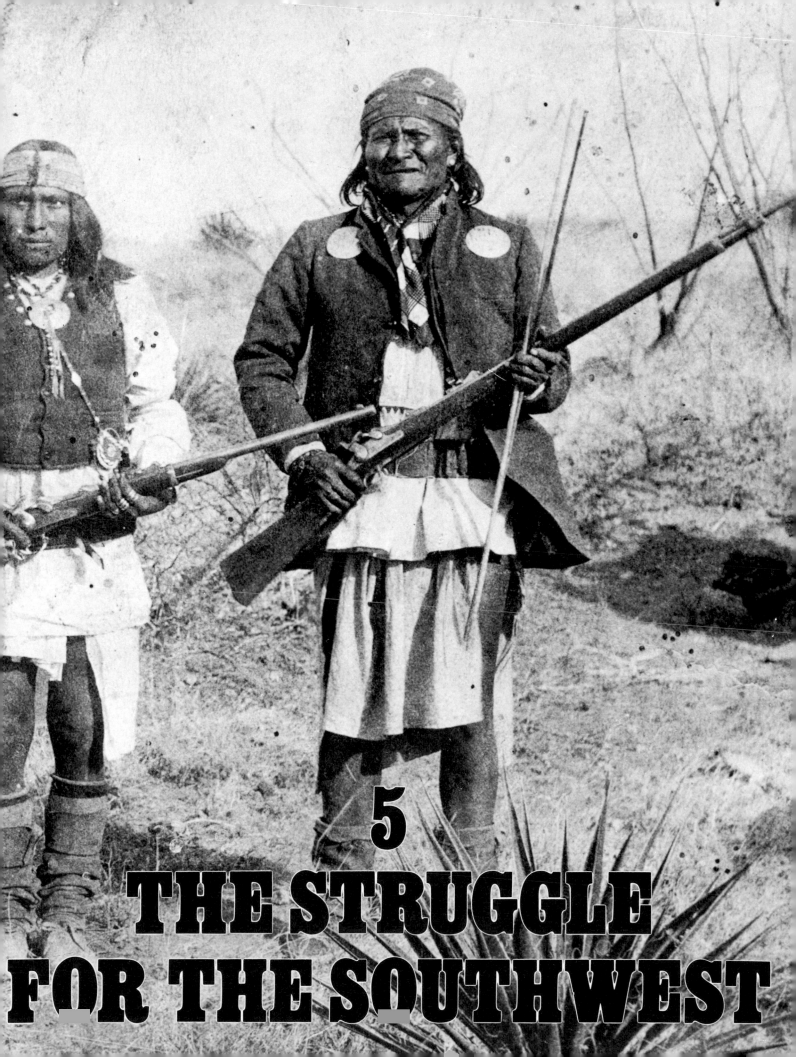

5
THE STRUGGLE
FOR THE SOUTHWEST

The old Kiowa chief, guarded by three soldiers and in handcuffs, sat in an open wagon. His name was Setangya, though he was known to the Americans as Satank. Suddenly he started to sing, sometimes ducking his head under a blanket. He was singing his death song, the song of the warrior society known as the Society of the Ten Bravest, and under the blanket he was gnawing the flesh from his hands so as to slip the handcuffs off them. Under the blanket he had a knife, perhaps slipped to him by a friend or hidden in his clothes. Later, the Kiowa were to claim that he got it by magic.

Not for him a white man's prison. He leaped up, stabbed at the guard nearest him and seized a carbine from another guard. He was about to fire it when an officer rapped out an order and bullets tore into him. When he finally died, his body was flung into a ditch, and the wagon train moved on, bearing two other Kiowa leaders, Satanta and Big Tree, away from their people. It was 1871 and the wars for the south plains were reaching their climax. Later on, Satanta was to find freedom in suicide, hurling himself head first from a prison hospital window.

While the plains epic was being played out by Sioux, Cheyenne, and other fighting tribes, an even starker contest between Indians and whites was reaching its climax in the deserts, plains and mountains of the Southwest. It had been going on far longer than the Plains Wars, virtually ever since Coronado's expedition of 1540. It could almost be said that the story begins and ends with the Apache. A century after the Coronado expedition of 1540, Apache were clashing with the Spaniards, and more than 200 years later their long struggle finally ended when the last hostile band surrendered in 1886.

The word Apache means enemy in Zuñi, the word Comanche means the same in Ute. The Comanche, those matchless horsemen, have been called the 'Lords of the South Plains.' They came down from the Rockies around 1700 and drove the eastern Apache out of Texas. The newcomers allied themselves firmly with a much smaller tribe, the Kiowa. The Apache had kinsmen, the Navaho, who were fierce warriors in the early days, as the Spaniards found out to their grief. Pitiless warfare on both sides was to last for four centuries. Other tribes felt the Apache-Navaho fury, notably the peace-loving Pueblo and the Apache-hating Pima. Only the Hopi remained aloof after a rebellion against the Spanish in 1680, and kept Apache and Navaho out of their high mesas.

By the middle of the 18th century, what is now the American Southwest had been abandoned to the Indians except on maps. Spain 'acquired' from the French the vast Louisiana Territory stretching from the Mississippi to the Rockies. France had pretended to own it on the strength of its occupancy by her valiant explorers, trappers and traders. The exchange came after the French had been defeated by Britain in the French and Indian War, but France handed the area over to Spain (their monarchs were related) rather than let it become British along with Canada. The Territory went back to France in a secret deal in 1800, but in 1803, Napoleon made his famous sale to Jefferson, the best land deal in history, when for a mere fifteen million dollars the Louisiana Territory was acquired by the young republic, doubling the size of the United States overnight. This is where the story of Americans in the Southwest really begins.

The inhabitants, Spaniards and Indians alike, had been more concerned with survival than international affairs, and, on the Indian side, with preventing their families from being captured and enslaved by the Mexicans. The Mexicans themselves secured their independence from Spain in 1821, and 15 years later, Texas, by now dominated by American settlers, secured its independence from Mexico after the heroic tragedy of the Alamo and the total defeat of the Mexicans at San Jacinto. Texas was to be an independent nation until she joined the United States in 1847.

Much of Texas was still Indian country, and one of the tribes which lived in it was the Kiowa.

There were only some 2,000 Kiowa, as opposed to 20,000 of their Comanche allies, but the fighting spirit of the smaller tribe was legendary. In 1833, however, a long period of misfortune started for the tribe, which ended in confinement on an Indian Territory reservation.

The misfortune happened in the Wichita Mountains in what is now southern Oklahoma.

Above: *Frontier Life—The Buffalo Hunt* **by Currier and Ives, 1862. Left: Two professional buffalo hunters. Below left: Buffalo hides piled high at Dodge City, Kansas, 1874.**

Most of the warriors had ridden off to fight the Ute, leaving behind in their camp their principal chief, Islandman, the older warriors, the women and the children. There were Osage warriors near—a buffalo carcass had one of their arrows in it to prove it—but Islandman allowed his people to split into several groups to go hunting, for buffalo as well as horses. While they were away, the main camp was attacked by Osage, and many women and children were killed and the tribe's sacred medicine idol, the taime, was lost to the enemy.

When the warriors returned, they were appalled, not least because their chief had failed his people and even fled. At a council many spoke, the older men beginning the oratory, and, finally, Little Mountain was chosen to lead the six divisions of the tribe. Much was expected of a Kiowa chief. Though not in charge of battle tactics, he had to have been a noted warrior who would now be respected by all, be generous, wise, and in every way a leader. Other tribes had other systems, but all would face the same basic problem from the 1830s on-

Brave Chief of the Pawnee tribe, by George Catlin, 1832. The painted hands on his chest indicate that he won a victory in close combat.

A Navajo Indian of Gallup, New Mexico. He is wearing the traditional native costume with necklace and silver belt.

Below: A Kiowa village, illustration by Baldwin Mollhausen. Right: Kiowa Chief Lone Wolf. Opposite top: A Kiowa couple, Trailing-the-Enemy and his wife. Below opposite: The peace-loving Kicking Bear.

ward, the problem other Indians had faced for so long—the white man.

So far, Kiowa experience in dealing with the whites had been confined to raiding the heavy freight wagons on the Santa Fe Trail. They had had the horse for a century, now they were taking the white man's goods. Traders had already supplied them with iron tools to replace the stone-tipped weapons of their ancestors, and in 1834, Little Mountain and his Kiowa had a productive meeting with Colonel Henry Dodge and his force of dragoons. The Indians were to stop the attacks on the Santa Fe Trail in return for trade concessions. A Kiowa girl, captured by the Osages, was given back to her own people by the whites, which made a fine impression. Better still, a visit to Fort Gibson in what is now eastern Oklahoma led to contacts with the Cherokee and other tribes, including the Osages. In exchange for a Kiowa horse, the Osages returned the sacred taime, and the result of all this was more than a decade of peace, at least on the Santa Fe Trail. It was still open season for raids on encroaching white Texans to the south.

As with so many tribes, things were never the same again for the Kiowa after the California gold strike of 1848. Instead of the occasional wagon train bound for Oregon, wagons seemed to come in endless lines, one disastrous side effect being cholera. And just 10 years after the California strikes came the Colorado strikes, which resulted in a sea of whites pouring across

Indian lands. Little Mountain had kept the peace, but no longer, and the Civil War and resulting withdrawal of troops saw travel along the Santa Fe Trail and points north become suicidal. News of Sand Creek increased the furious tempo of Indian attacks, Kiowa and Comanche taking ruthless vengeance on the interlopers.

Then disaster struck. Ex-mountain man Kit Carson and his New Mexico volunteers were ordered to attack the Kiowa and some Comanche allies in the Texas Panhandle. Valiantly as the Indians fought one freezing November day in 1864, they were no match for Carson's two 12-pounder howitzers and a white force backed up by 72 Ute and Jicarilla Apache. Little Mountain led his people as magnificently as Islandman had let them down, but the artillery turned the tide. It led to a peace conference in which the Kiowa accepted a reservation that included what became southwestern Oklahoma and the Texas Panhandle. Though their finest buffalo range was included, they had little realized what reservation life entailed, especially that the buffalo herd would decrease in numbers. Had not the whites promised food, tools and clothing?

Little Mountain died shortly after the treaty was signed and before the full implications of the treaty, with all its talk of farming, had sunk into Kiowa minds. And as so often happened, in what was always the worst crisis to face a tribe, the Kiowa split, as the Sioux had split, into war and peace parties.

The leading war chief, Satank, was too old to be principal chief and the post went to Satanta, or White Bear, who was prepared to get along with the whites for what the tribe could extract from them, yet still continue raiding. The peace party wanted Kicking Bear. A man in between, Lone Wolf, was chosen.

In 1867, a great council was held at Medicine Lodge, Kansas, the Kiowa being joined by Comanche, Cheyenne and Arapaho. All the Kiowa leaders were present, Satanta making a great impression on newspaperman Henry M Stanley, later of 'Doctor Livingstone, I presume?' fame. The chief strongly condemned the destruction of the buffalo by soldiers on their way

to the council and it was swiftly banned. After more stirring recitals of wrongs, however, all the Kiowa leaders signed except Lone Wolf.

The Kiowa and Comanche were now on a smaller reservation. In return they were to be given $25,000 a year for buying useful goods and, more importantly, hunting rights north of the Washita River were to be retained.

Naturally, the rights were rapidly removed— by Sherman, supported by Grant—and naturally the money due them was often late. The Kiowa were now deeply divided about policy. With Satanta preaching war, Kicking Bear, as a noted warrior, was in the impossible position of being a peace advocate. At the 1870 Sun Dance he was called a coward and was forced to prove himself. He then led a raid into Texas and at one point headed a charge straight at troopers of the Sixth Cavalry and spectacularly impaled a trooper on his lance. As a result of this episode his arguments for peace were heard with more respect.

The next year, the Kiowa, though not Kicking Bear, were out again, led by Satank, Big Tree and the prophet, Sky Walker. His prophecies were less than sound. The Indians saw officers in an open coach escorted by only 17 men, but Sky Walker told them a better target would soon come into view. So they left unmolested one of their supreme enemies, General Sherman.

A day later, they ferociously attacked a wagon train, one man being tied to his wagon and, after having his tongue cut out, burned to death.

Soon after this, the chiefs were at their agency, drawing rations, and Satanta frankly admitted to the agent, a Quaker named Tatum, that he had led the raid. Tatum was then treated to a long and accurate list of the wrongs done to the Kiowa, but Satanta's confession was passed on to Sherman, who ordered that the chiefs be tried for murder. On their way to their trial in Texas, Satank died, as previously related. Big Tree and Satanta were tried in front of Indian-hating frontiersmen at Jacksboro. Satanta proposed to withdraw his warriors from Texas if he was freed, and delivered a grim warning of the consequences if he was not, but he and Big Tree were sentenced to hang.

The judge suggested to Governor Davis of Texas that they be sentenced to life imprisonment and hard labor instead, and the pair were sent to Huntsville prison. Kicking Bear, still trying to keep the peace, and Lone Wolf, desisting at last from warlike postures, swore to keep the peace if the prisoners were freed, and in 1873 they were released. Sherman was furious.

Yet how could such chiefs keep the peace when Indian lands were being invaded and the slaughter of the buffalo was reaching new levels? 1874 saw raids by Kiowa, their Comanche friends, Cheyenne, and Arapaho. President Grant authorized Sherman, now General of the Army, to strike back. Any Indian not reporting every Thursday to his agency was to be regarded as hostile, and the Indians were subjected to a five-pronged attack. Kicking Bear reached new heights of leadership trying to keep the Kiowa at peace, succeeding with the majority, but not with Satanta and Big Tree. Finally, they too, came in. They swore that they

Opposite: The Cherokee chief Stalking Turkey. His portrait was painted when he was in London in 1762. This page: Petalesharo, a chief of the Pawnees, as painted by the artist Charles Bird King in the year 1821.

Center: Colonel Nelson A Miles of the United States Army. Left: Christopher 'Kit' Carson, the famous fur trapper, guide and Indian-fighting soldier. Right: Colonel Ranald MacKenzie, who was the commander of the US Fourth Cavalry.

had only left to visit friends off the reservation, but they were arrested and taken to Fort Sill. Satanta was sent back to Huntsville where, in 1878, he died, as previously described. Meanwhile, Kicking Bear was told to select the most untameable hostiles for transportation to prison in Fort Marion, Florida. His task was as invidious as it was impossible, but he tried to spare those he felt would be most useful to the tribe in the times ahead. As the prisoners were being loaded into wagons, he publicly stated that he would try to get them sent back.

Sky Walker, who, with Lone Wolf, was one of the prisoners, spoke bitterly to Kicking Bear and told him he would not live long. On the journey he prayed for his enemy's death, and only a few days after the prisoners had left, Kicking Bear did indeed die of mysterious stomach pains. The army doctor stated that

death was caused by strychnine. As for Sky Walker, he died in Florida.

The prisoners suffered in Florida's humid climate, first in dungeons, then in barracks. But their keeper, Lieutenant Pratt, was a man of honor who tried to help them in every way to adjust to a new life. Three years later, they were returned to the West. There they were to be led by Big Tree and live along Rainy Mountain Creek in Indian Territory. Big Tree became a Sunday school teacher and a deacon. Such was the fate of the Kiowa, a small tribe and a valiant one, whose story typifies the stormy period when they and the whites so tragically clashed.

When J T Farnham wrote about the Comanche in his *Travels in the Great Western Prairies*, published in 1839, he went in for superlatives. They were 'Spartans of the Plains', their 'incomparable horsemanship, their incredible courage, the unequalled rapidity with which they load and discharge their fire-arms, and their insatiable hatred make the enmity of these Indians more dreadful than that of any other tribe of aborigines.'

The Comanche had broken away from their Shoshone kinsmen in the Rocky Mountains around 1700 to become the lords of the south plains. Early in the 19th century there were some 20,000 of them. Unlike their Kiowa friends, they had no principal chief, but five main bands who could do anything they wanted except fight fellow Comanche.

They were traders as well as fighters, horses, not surprisingly, being important goods, for these Indians were generally regarded as the supreme horsemen of all the North American tribes.

The Comanche harried the Spanish settlements down the years, though the Spaniards had one major Indian ally, the Lipan Apache. When the American settlers won Texas in the 1830s, the Comanche found themselves faced with a more implacable enemy. White records tell of Comanche atrocities, of the horrors endured by surviving captives, but, like so much in the story of the Indian Wars, generalizations are suspect. There was no room in a Comanche camp for prisoners as such, so males were usually killed and women taken, raped perhaps, and sometimes married into the tribe. Children were often adopted into it.

Comanche expected no quarter and gave none. Torture was not inevitable, though angry Comanche could torture with the best, but whites who showed valor were much admired, and, if they became captives, might then be treated well for their bravery. White atrocities to Comanche were naturally less publicized.

The very first war between the Comanche and the newly independent Texans had historic results. The Indians captured Cynthia Ann Parker, aged nine, after her grandfather had been butchered and her grandmother tortured. She soon adapted herself into the Indian life-style, like so many young captives down the centuries, and she married Peta Nocona. The Comanche birthrate was dangerously low, but Cynthia Ann gave the tribe three children, including the most famous and the greatest of his tribe, Quanah Parker. When white hunters offered to ransom her in the 1850s, she turned down the offer.

The Comanche, who would ride 100 miles without food or rest, always planned for their retreat as well as their attack, keeping fresh mounts ready. The Texans raised the Texas Rangers as early as 1835 to combat the Comanche and protect their long frontier, and

Above: *The Emigrants* by Frederic Remington. The driver is attempting to hold off an attack by Indians. Left: *A Peril of the Plains* showing the horsemanship of the Comanche Indians. Illustration by Frederic Remington.

when Texas became part of the United States in 1847, the army built forts, but failed to fill them with cavalrymen. Infantry against the Comanche were useless. Better from the white point of view was the cholera which hit the plains along with the Forty-Niners. Whites could be replaced, but not decimated Indian bands.

In 1860, Rangers swept down on a village when most warriors were hunting buffalo. One of the prisoners taken was Cynthia Ann Parker, who was identified by her uncle and was taken with her daughter to the family home in east Texas. Quanah, now a rising warrior, could never find where she was held. It was not until the Medicine Lodge Treaty of 1867 that he discovered she had time and again tried to escape to her Comanche people until, after her daugh-

A collection of artifacts of the Plains Indians. This grouping is from a painting made by Karl Bodmer.

numbers when set against the growing flood of whites.

The Kwahadie were among the Indians who boycotted the Medicine Lodge council, though the government, with nine Comanche chiefs' signatures on the treaty, considered that the tribe was virtually tamed. As we have seen, the government's promises were soon forgotten and, meanwhile, those Comanche who had refused to sign kept fighting, helped by warriors who left the reservation from time to time, especially when white promises were broken.

Into the arena in 1871 stepped 31-year-old Colonel Ranald S Mackenzie, considered by Ulysses S Grant to be the most promising young officer in the army. He took up his post at the head of the Fourth Cavalry at Fort Richardson, Texas. No believer in spit and polish, he was a firm advocate of harsh discipline and rapidly turned the Fourth into the finest cavalry regiment in the army, able to fight as guerrillas against matchless guerrilla opponents. In September, he marched against the Kwahadie on the Staked Plains. Quanah Parker and his braves launched lightning attacks on the troops, but refused a large-scale battle. Wintry weather finally ended the campaign, which had at least allowed the troops to gain vivid experience against the most militant of the lords of the south plains.

In March 1872, Mackenzie was back in action. The Kotsoteka Comanche were defeated and the survivors gave up the struggle for good, settling on the reservation. Meanwhile, Mackenzie was finding evidence of just how well the Kiowa and Comanche had been supplied down the years with arms and whiskey by the New Mexican traders known as Comancheros, who took Indian plunder in exchange. From then on, the traders' days were numbered.

Those were the days of freedom for Quanah and his band, though their raiding was cut down to prevent retaliation upon Comanche captives by whites. This was misinterpreted by the whites, who assumed that the Comanche had given up the struggle, and the prisoners were released. The result was that Quanah and his warriors took to the warpath again and Mackenzie resumed his offensive patrols.

ter died in 1864, she had starved herself to death.

Back in 1860, with Quanah's brother dead of disease and his father dead probably from a wound, he set out to join the Kwahadie Comanche in western Texas. With the Civil War raging, Comanche and Kiowa terrorized the undefended frontier, but their spectacular successes could not disguise their paucity of

The situation was dramatically changed the following year not by the military, but by the descent on the Texas Panhandle of an army of buffalo hunters, who turned the area into a giant abbatoir. Better weapons now enabled a real marksman, armed with a Sharps rifle, to kill over 200 buffalo a day. In 1872–73, 1,250,000 hides had been shipped east by rail, and, with the killing rate up, it could only be a matter of time before the herds vanished altogether. The Indians saw the innumerable carcasses left to rot.

The government, of course, had completely failed to keep the hunters out, while Sheridan spoke for many when he rejoiced in their work, which would result in the plains being covered 'with speckled cattle and the festive cowboy.'

The Indians' mood was anything but festive, and a hard core of Comanche, Kiowa, Arapaho and Cheyenne joined forces in a war of revenge for the deaths of so many braves, and for the destruction of the buffalo herds. Being the warriors they were, it gave them a chance to excel yet again in action, but this time there was a new edge to their fury.

It was heightened by the appearance of a Comanche Medicine Man named Isatai. At times of supreme crisis, the Indians were only too prone to believe in such men, and this prophet had successfully predicted that a comet then in the sky would disappear in five days, then be followed by a long summer drought. His other predictions were more dangerous. Having, so he said, been up to heaven, he claimed that he could belch up wagonloads of ammunition and that the braves and their horses would be invulnerable against white men's bullets. An attack on the whites would therefore succeed and bring the buffalo back.

Unlike many Plains Indians, the Comanche did not hold Sun Dances, but their prophet now urged them to do so. When it was over, an attack was planned on the buffalo hunters' base, a trading post called Adobe Walls on the North Canadian River. Quanah Parker led some 700 warriors from four tribes to this spot, Isatai spreading disastrous good cheer as they rode, proclaiming how he would stop all the white men's guns. Among the chiefs who rode that day were the Kiowa, Lone Wolf and Satanta.

There were 28 men and one woman at Adobe Walls, lodged in three buildings some distance from each other. They had high-powered rifles, but they might have been taken by surprise and wiped out if things had gone the Indians' way. Accounts vary, but it seems that James Hanrahan, the saloon keeper, suspecting that Indians might be near, fired a shot, then said that the noise was the ridgepole of his saloon splitting. It certainly had the effect of getting enough men up and about to prop up the pole, enjoy a drink, and spot the approaching braves. Inevitably, with the element of surprise gone, the chances of an Indian success against a sound defensive position were drastically decreased. The warriors, discovering all too soon that their prophet was a fraud, charged again and again, withdrawing from time to time in a vain effort to make the whites run out of ammunition. Quanah had his horse shot out from under him, while his warriors were being picked off at long range by the hunters' buffalo guns with their telescopic sights. Finally, the attackers gave up, Quanah saving Isatai from a severe flogging. His total disgrace was enough.

There were 13 Indian bodies for the whites to decapitate. They then stuck the heads on poles. How many more died is not known, for other dead must have been taken away. The whites lost only three. Quanah Parker was never blamed for the defeat, indeed his valor was prodigious in the battle, but Adobe Walls was a crushing blow to Indian morale. Many Indians now went on the rampage in Texas and Kansas, killing settlers and travelers, attacking army mail parties and, in the case of Lone Wolf, avenging the death of his son and nephew by a daring ambush on a group of Texas Rangers. Colonel Mackenzie and 600 men were ordered to seek out and destroy Quanah Parker and his Kwahadie, while four other columns headed for less lethal targets.

Yet Mackenzie was lucky, for thanks to his scouts, he came upon the mighty Palo Duro Canyon on 28 September 1874, a chasm virtually unknown to whites since Coronado saw it in the 1540s. Kiowa, Comanche and Cheyenne were there with their families, though not Quanah Parker, who, if he had been, would no doubt have posted sentries. Into the canyon went the troopers, and though many of the Indians escaped, their winter food and dwellings were destroyed and their huge horse herd was captured.

The other columns were gradually rounding up the hostiles and, finally, on 2 June 1875, Quanah led his surviving Kwahadie into Fort Sill three months after Lone Wolf and his Kiowa had given up. He and Mackenzie met face to face. Neither could have imagined that the great chief had 35 more years of life in which, without ever losing his self-respect, he would be as triumphant in peace as he had been so often in war. After difficult years of adjustment for his people, he was to become as clever at land deals as he had been in setting an ambush. He spoke English well, and armed with a letter written by his Indian agent stating who he was, he found his mother's family, stayed a while with them, and typically, studied farming with them. He then returned to his Indian people.

He became an Indian who would be at home in Washington and became a personal friend of President Teddy Roosevelt. On the reservation, he had a large house and eight wives. He was a lawman for a time and a notable judge, and though he never abandoned his Comanche faith, he respected and supported the clergy. He hunted with Roosevelt on Indian land and rode beside him in Roosevelt's Inaugural procession. When he died in 1911, he was buried beside his

Right: Satanta, or Set-tain-te, also known as White Bear, 1870. Below: Custer demands that Satanta bring his Kiowa to Fort Cobb.

mother, dressed in the full glory of a chief of the Comanche Nation, whose supreme hero he had been.

During the war with Mexico, when American troops marched into Las Vegas, New Mexico, in August 1846, their commander, General Stephen Kearny, made a speech to the populace. After expressing suitable sentiments about the benefits of American rule, he went on to the subject of Indian attacks. 'From the American Government you have never received protection,' he said. 'The Apaches and Navahos come down from the mountains and carry off your

Opposite: Big Elk of the Omahas, painted by George Catlin, 1832. His black face indicates he has killed an enemy. Left: Geronimo, the warrior leader of the Chiricahua Apaches.

sheep, and even your women, whenever they please.' He went on to say how things would now change.

The Navaho were more organized as a tribe than their Apache cousins. There were perhaps 12,000 of them at this time. They farmed as well as hunted, and raised sheep, while in their stronghold, the spectacular Canyon de Chelly, they were proud of their peach trees. They were indeed raiders, cutting deep into Mexico as well as attacking the Pueblo Indians. Women and children were carried north. Yet as the Mexicans were doing exactly the same things, and had been for centuries, it is better not to assign blame but face the situation as it was in the late 1840s when the United States annexed Arizona and New Mexico. They rounded off both southward to their present boundaries with the Gadsden Purchase of 1853.

The Navaho were famed for their fine blankets, their clothing and their silverware, though they lived simply enough in earth huts called hogans. Their sand paintings were inspired by those of the Pueblo, while their style of warfare was closer to that of the Plains Indians than that of their Apache cousins, whose warfare, truly Spartan in its iron hardness, had a dedicated ruthlessness about it and a logic that was unique in the history of the Indian Wars.

The Mexican War ended in 1848 and 1000 troops marched into the Ninth Military Department, as New Mexico was styled. The atmosphere was tense. The year before, a rebellion by the Taos Indians, encouraged by Mexicans, had resulted in American lives being lost, while in 1849, Forty-Niners heading for California behaved toward the Indians as they were to behave toward California's Indians—treating them as if they were vermin. Naturally, the peaceful Pueblo Indians suffered most.

The American troops, divided into small units, launched attacks on a number of tribes, including the Navaho. A Navaho chief was killed and a treaty made on the edge of the Canyon de Chelly. Yet there was no peace, especially after raids by Jicarilla Apache and Ute.

In 1851, Colonel Edwin V Sumner took over the Department, the same 'Bull' Sumner whom we met in the last chapter. In his determined manner, he moved his men out of luxurious Santa Fe, set up a supply and ordnance depot which was to become the key post of Fort Union, then had Fort Defiance built in Navaho country. Other forts sprang up, and relations between the strong-willed Sumner and the civilian authorities became more than somewhat strained. When he left the territory in 1852, he had so improved the army's defensive system that future Indian attacks would be much easier to combat. His successors continued building forts, while 'Bull' Sumner went north to fight other Indians.

The Navaho remained at peace, apart from sporadic raids, until 1858. There was a fine officer, Major Kendrick, in command of Fort Defiance, and Henry Dodge was a distinguished and honorable Indian agent. Inevitably, however, the whites could not understand that Navaho chiefs were unable to control all their people—the classic 'democracy spells anarchy' syndrome—so white hostility remained constant. Incidents were smoothed over, but the death of Dodge, killed by Apache, led to real trouble.

It came in 1858, when a Navaho in an ugly mood killed an officer's black slave in Fort Defiance. The man had just got in his way, there was nothing personal. A minor tragedy led to a short war which had Navaho territory swarming with soldiers; there were so many of them that what seemed like a solid peace settlement was signed on Christmas Day of the same year.

Navaho leaders like Manuelito had no reason to be satisfied with the situation. Colonel Bonneville was in command at Santa Fe and, with the Superintendant of Indian Affairs in Santa Fe, James Collins, was responsible for the Christmas Day peace settlement on the white side, but they had held back 21 Navaho as hostages. To the Navaho it must have seemed part of the same pattern that branded them as noncitizens to be punished as outlaws if they raided Mexicans, yet did not help them if Mexicans stole their women and children. Tension rapidly built up after the Navaho were informed that their livestock could not use pasture near the fort, which, as the Indians had no fences, was an order hard to obey. The result was an official slaughter of the Navaho horse herd in the area. Raids and counter raids built up to an all-out attack on Fort Defiance before dawn on 30 April 1860 by more than 1000 Indians. Using a few ancient guns and their bows and arrows, they forced the sentries to retreat and took several buildings, then fired at the soldiers as they erupted from their barracks rooms. Once the Americans had managed to form up and begin firing, the chances of an Indian victory vanished, but when the warriors retreated at dawn, they had every reason to be pleased with their assault.

The only effect it had on the military was to spur them into offensive action. Colonel Edward Canby, who was later to be murdered by the Modoc, rode out with six companies of cavalry and nine of infantry, more than 600 men, plus a strong band of Ute auxiliaries and a force of Mexican scouts. The month-long campaign was an almost total failure. Though some crops and flocks of sheep were destroyed, the area was experiencing its second year of drought, making conditions hellish for soldiers and horses alike. And Navaho warriors kept harrying the command's flanks. Canby returned to Fort Defiance.

Yet, though he had failed, the Navaho, too, had suffered. Morale was not raised by constant pressure from troops, their own farming had been interrupted, horses and sheep had been killed. It seemed a good moment to try for peace again. A meeting was held at the newly established Fort Fauntleroy, named for the new Department commander and situated some 30 miles south of Defiance. It was attended by Herrero Grande, Manuelito, Delgadito, and other leading Navaho, Canby being the ranking American representative. On 21 February 1861, Herrero Grande was chosen as head chief by his people, peace was the watchword on all sides, and the new chief stated that thieving Navaho, the *ladrones,* would be expelled from the tribe. This was not so much a controversial promise as one hard to implement. Inevitably the more warlike elements tended to sympathize with the outcasts.

The outbreak of the Civil War in April seriously affected the situation in the Southwest as elsewhere. Some of the Bluecoats left to ex-

Top to bottom: A Navajo man, photographed in the 1880s. Navajo Indians with their sheep herd. An unmarried girl and her mother of the Arizona Hopis.

change their costumes for gray, including Fauntleroy, the fort named after him being renamed Fort Lyon. Canby found himself opposing, then turning back, a Confederate force led by an officer who had served under him, Henrey Sibley, who was now a Confederate brigadier general.

In September 1861, a tragedy occurred. The Navaho were in the habit of calling at the renamed fort to enjoy horse racing with the garrison, who were New Mexico Volunteers. The races took place when the Indians were collecting rations from the agent and doing some trading. The big race on 13 September was between Manuelito on a Navaho horse and an officer on a quarterhorse. Betting was heavy, but almost as soon as the race started, the Indian horse ran off the track, because Manuelito was quite unable to control it. It seems that his bridle rein had been slashed and the Navahos understandably cried foul. The all-soldier judges' panel refused to allow the race to be rerun, and the soldiers went off happily to the fort to collect their winnings, pursued by angry Indians.

A Navaho, trying to enter the fort, was shot. What happened next has been disputed, the bloodbath apart, but there is no reason to doubt the account of Sergeant Nicholas Hodt, who told his story in 1865—by which time he was a captain. This was a very different story as compared to the official whitewash of the camp commander, Colonel Chavez, by Captain Evans of the Sixth Cavalry.

Hodt revealed how Indian men, women and children were shot and bayoneted and how the commandant ordered mountain howitzers to be used on them, despite protests by the sergeant in charge of the guns. The Indians rushed away, and were soon engaged on raiding the settlements once again. The fragile peace was broken. Hodt revealed how the only Indians still at the fort were a few women, 'Favorites of the officers.' Chavez sent some of these women to talk to the chiefs, who flogged them for their pains.

The following spring, the Californian Volun-

Top: Apache scouts on a US Army campaign in Arizona in the 1880s. Bottom left: Mickey Free, an army scout. Bottom right: Al Sieber, chief of Scouts, with some of his Apaches in 1883.

teers marched into New Mexico under a very tough leader, Colonel James H Carleton. Able, keen and ruthless, he was on his way to become the new department commander. His 'Column from California' had retaken Tucson, Arizona without a fight, the Confederate company there having evacuated the town. Now,

with 1800 men, he was marching on Santa Fe, where, from the white point of view, he was badly needed, the campaigns against the Indians having been shelved because of the Confederate scare.

Unlike most army officers, he understood Indian guerrilla warfare, and acted accordingly, and, tyrannical as he was, he held the respect of his men. He had shown his qualities against the Jicarilla Apache in 1855, learning from his guide, Kit Carson. Finding the veteran scout in New Mexico, he made him a colonel, and launched a campaign against the Mescalero Apache. They were to be driven to a woody spot on the Pecos River, where a new fort called Fort Sumner was built in the heart of what was known as the Bosque Redondo. The choice was death for all warriors or a forced relocation, as the whites wanted their fertile land. Carleton's original order stated that Indian men 'are to be slain whenever and wherever they can be found', which was too much for Carson, though not for a Captain Graydon, who managed to fill one Mescalero band with liquor, then shoot them all down. By January 1863, most surviving Mescalero Apache had settled down at Bosque Redondo, a few warriors apart, and, though anyone trying to go home would risk being shot, the treatment of the Mescalero on the reservation could have been far worse. It had taken just three months, and was a dress rehearsal for a major campaign against the Navaho.

In April 1863, Carleton spelled out his terms for the Navaho to two peace chiefs, Delgadito and Barboncito, and grim terms they were. All 'friendly' Navaho must leave their homeland and settle at Bosque Redondo. Barboncito stated that he would not go so far away from home. On 23 June, Carleton ordered Colonel Chavez to summon Delgadito and Barboncito to the newly built Fort Wingate in eastern New Mexico. He was to repeat the ultimatum and tell them that they could have until 20 July to come in, 'they and all those who belong to what they call the peace party', and after that day every Navaho seen 'will be considered as hostile and treated accordingly,' and that from that day the door now open would be closed to them.

Naturally, no Navaho gave themselves up, and as the tribe was far larger than the Mescalero, there seemed every likelihood of a bitter campaign. Carson wanted no part of it, being no Indian-hater and now a man of some prosperity as well as fame. Carleton, however, had a way of getting what he wanted, and he got Carson. His 1000 strong regiment was to be based at Fort Canby, as Fort Defiance was now renamed, and Colonel Chavez was to be at Fort Wingate. Though at first the main Indian losses were their herds and crops, a new factor arose when old enemies of the Navaho—Ute, Pueblo and Hopi—began to act against them. So did citizen bands of raiders.

The first to crack under the strain of Carleton's aggressive policy was the band led by Delgadito and Barboncito, some 500 strong. Instead of being allowed to settle near Fort Wingate, they were forced to go to Bosque Redondo, Carleton seeing to it that these first captives were well treated in order to encourage the others. And now he turned his attention to the main target, the Canyon de Chelly, which Carson was ordered to invade.

At the head of his 389 officers and men, Carson set out from a frosty Fort Canby on 6 January 1864, heading for the western entrance of the Canyon. Meanwhile, Captain Albert Pfeiffer, whose wife's death at the hands of Apache had turned him into a ferocious Indian hater, set out with two companies for the eastern approach.

Despite heavy snow and a delay in finding a safe passage to the bottom of the Canyon, Carson and his men had little trouble, while Pfeiffer fared only slightly worse. He and his troops had wood and stones hurled down on them, but they destroyed a vast amount of property—hogans, herds and food—killed a few Navaho and rounded up some women and children. Carson's men also killed some before the two forces linked up. The high spot of the campaign was the total destruction of the Navaho's beloved peach trees, over 500 of them.

Now many hundreds of Navaho were ready to surrender at Forts Wingate and Canby, and soon the numbers ran into thousands. It was a time for yet more Trails of Tears, though in Navaho history the name is the Long Walk of the Navaho. Late in 1864, more than 8000 Navaho, three-quarters of the tribe, had been driven to their new 'home'. The majority of deaths on the trail had occurred the previous March in grim winter weather. Carleton, the hero of New Mexico, looked forward to a happy time when the Navaho would all be Christians, complete with new habits and ideas, in their arid new home, while his adjutant general considered the Long

Walk 'an interesting but a touching sight'. As for Carson, he was made a brevet brigadier general of volunteers.

Everyone seemed to agree that the new homeland of the tribe was suitable, everyone except Apache agent Michael Steck, who noted that there was not enough arable land for the Navaho with their flocks and herds, and also objected to locating them alongside Apache. Kinsmen they might be, but the two groups had hated each other for a century.

Manuelito and a hard core of warriors were still at large, plus some women and children, and as the months went by, more and more Navaho left the reservation. The failure of the grain crop in 1865 was yet another factor in the nightmare. Finally, on 1 September 1866, Manuelito and 23 warriors surrendered and soon after, Barboncito, who had broken out, brought 21 more in.

It was at this time that General Carleton left New Mexico. Meanwhile, A B Norton, the new superintendent at Bosque Redondo, was appalled by the soil, the water and the reservation generally, as well as its colossal cost to the nation. The Apache and Navaho were getting along badly, as experts knew they would, and the whole affair was clearly a total disaster. There is no reason to doubt that Carleton was speaking the truth as he saw it when he predicted that the Navaho would form 'the happiest and most delightfully located pueblo of Indians in New Mexico—perhaps in the United States,' but he managed to be 100 percent wrong.

General Sherman was to react differently. Others had seen the reservation and been horrified; he was shocked and had the power to act. Having carefully explained how whites punished those who broke the law, he told the Indians that if they signed a new treaty they could go home. The treaty was signed on 1 June 1868 and home they went. They had lost some of their best land, but they were home indeed. Naturally, New Mexicans, except those near the Canyon who saw pickings in the form of federal money, were highly displeased, but, as Sherman noted, they and Carleton were 'half-crazy' on the subject. And, of course, life would still be hard even though the Navaho were home. Yet in the dark years ahead for the American Indians, they were some of the very few lucky ones, even though the Long Walk and its aftermath were seared into tribal memory.

The plains were peaceful for most of the 1880s, however crushed and wretched their Indian inhabitants might be. Only in one part of the United States was there warfare, almost constant and always ferocious. The place was the Southwest and the warriors were the Apache.

Their implacable enmity toward the Spaniards, and toward many other Indian tribes, has already been noted. It is both useless and impossible to assign blame for the centuries of hostility, but it is fair to try to discover just why the Apache became not only so implacable but often so fiendishly cruel.

First, there was a background of several centuries of having their women and children enslaved by Spaniards and Mexicans. When Americans took over the Southwest, the enslavement continued, along with enforced prostitution. Apache women could savagely torture captives, tormenting them like fiends, but how much of this was revenge not just for men killed but for children lost to them? Twenty-nine children were seized in one incident in 1871, and it cannot be coincidence that mutilation of the dead by Apache had become far more widespread in the 1860s. Yet when the Americans arrived, they had been welcomed by the Apache. Mutual hostility, however, soon developed.

Naturally, treachery under a flag of truce and massacres of Apache enflamed hatred, but it was steady, planned genocide that was a sure guarantee of provoking the most terrible revenge. The scalp hunters who killed Apache—or any other Indians they found—for bounty money were a repulsive breed. A law was passed in the state of Chihuahua in 1837 which offered 100 pesos (roughly $100) for a warrior's scalp. Soon the state of Sonora was offering 50 pesos for a woman's scalp and 25 pesos for a child's scalp. Europeans since Spanish times, had paid for scalps in certain periods, but the scalp hunters of the Southwest brought their ghastly trade to new heights of brutishness.

All this is not to deny that Mexicans suffered so much from the Apache that their hatred is understandable. As for the Americans, Indian-white hostility had an awful inevitability about it.

The true Apache—as opposed to tribes who had the word added to their names—Apache Mohave, Apache Yuma—were perhaps some 6000 strong. They were even less of a 'nation' than the Comanche and, unlike them, they were sometimes prepared to fight each other.

The Chiricahua lived in what is now southeastern Arizona, though there was another band of Chiricahua in the mountains below the border, these being called the Nednhi, or Enemy People. The Jicarilla roamed over southern Colorado and northern New Mexico. The Western Apache were the Tonto, Piñalero and Coyotero. They lived in central Arizona and, unlike the other divisions of the tribe, raised some crops. The Mimbreño (Mimbres) lived in southwestern New Mexico. There were two tribes, the Mimbreño and the Warm Springs, or Ojo Caliente, bands, and they were closely linked by marriage to the Chiricahua. The Mescalero roamed central and southern New Mexico. The mescal in their name does not refer to the alcoholic drink used in the Southwest, but a valuable food, the roasted leaves of the agave plant. It is highly nutritious. The Mogollon got their name from the Mogollon Mountains on the Arizona-New Mexico border. In the mid-19th century, the White Mountain Apache and the Aravaipa were situated to the north of the Chiricahua. The Apache simply called themselves Dine, The People. Apache is a corrupt version of the Zuñi Indian word for enemy.

The Apache were brilliant bowmen up to a range of some 150 yards. They used clubs, knives and lances, and, sometimes, poisoned arrows. They naturally adopted firearms and were always trying to get ammunition. Reports suggest they were not good marksmen. As they managed to keep much of the Southwest in a state of panic for so long, it was as well for the whites that their shooting was less than first rate. Some of the finest guerrilla fighters known to history, they could live like lizards in their stupendously dramatic land of deserts and canyons and mountains, much of which even today is too rugged for any but the most dauntless traveler.

Their legendary powers of endurance were taught them when they were young. Before sunrise throughout the year, boys were expected to swim and run, then, when the sun came up, they ran up a hill and back with a mouthful of water to see that they breathed properly through their nostrils. Girls swam and

Left: Cynthia Ann Parker with her daughter Prairie Flower. Right: Quanah Parker, her Comanche son.

Geronimo, the great Apache warrior leader.

ran, too. A warrior could cover 70 miles in a day on foot. As in most tribes, boys were trained for war in childhood games, yet the results among the Apache reached epic heights.

The Apache were masters of ambush and stealth, which made up for the fact that there were never enough of them. Public heroics meant little to them, but if trapped, especially with their families, they would fight with extreme ferocity. The few white men, including a number of army officers, who got to know the Apache, had a high opinion of them. General Crook's adjutant, Captain John Bourke wrote: 'No Indian has more virtues and none has been more truly ferocious when aroused . . . In peace he has commanded respect for keen-sighted intelligence, good fellowship, warmth of feeling for his friends and impatience of wrong.'

The countdown to the Americans' wars with the Apache was as savage as anything in the harsh decades to come. The few Americans in the Southwest had been on reasonable terms with the Apache, then, in 1837, a massacre occurred.

Juan José, a Mimbreño who may have been educated for the priesthood, became an implac-

able enemy of the Mexicans when his father was murdered. A singularly repulsive part-time scalp hunter, James Johnson, got to know him and made a contract with the Mexican authorities. He then lured the chief and his people to a feast held near the Santa Rita copper mines in what is now southern New Mexico. The best-known account, Captain John Carey Cremony's, written long after the event, has nearly 400 killed by cannon, guns, clubs and knives. The more likely version, by a man named Wilson who was nearby and talked to eyewitnesses, has less than a tenth as many killed. Whatever the truth, it was a horrible crime. Johnson lived to old age.

A survivor of the massacre was brought to the fore, Mangas Coloradas, a warrior whom many regard as the greatest of all Apache leaders of the 19th century. Born between 1790 and 1795, he was well over six feet tall and highly intelligent. Now he was to lead a campaign of vengeance.

An expedition of 22 trappers was wiped out, while the citizens of Santa Rita, near starvation because supplies were not getting through to them, were forced to leave and were butchered, only a handful surviving the massacre. The Apache raids on Mexico grew more and more destructive, and by the time that war broke out between the United States and Mexico in 1846, the condition of northern Mexico—thanks to Comanche as well as Apache—was pitiful. And all the while, a notorious scalp hunter named Kirker was killing Apache, and Mexicans, too, when it suited him. He claimed to have killed 487 Apache for their scalps. How many were actually Apache is not known.

Mangas Coloradas hoped to ally himself to the Americans who entered the West under Kearny in 1846, but his offer was turned down. All the while, his power grew. Like the statesman he was, he gave one of his daughters in marriage to Cochise, already the renowned chief of the Chiricahua, the others, though the evidence is conflicting, to another Apache and to a Navaho. His longed-for friendship with the Americans did not survive a brutal flogging by some miners whom he had been watching in Piños Altos as they searched for gold.

Cochise was still at peace with the Americans, though his warriors rode regularly into Mexico. Some of his men were even helping cut wood for the Butterfield Stage Line post beside a spring in Apache Pass. But Cochise was driven onto the warpath against the whites.

The sequence of events was as follows: On 27 January 1861, John Ward's ranch in the Sonoita Valley was raided by Apache while he was away. Interrupted by two Americans, they made off with 20 head of cattle and his stepson, Felix Telles, later to be the noted interpreter-scout, Mickey Free.

Word reached Fort Buchanan, and the next day Lieutenant Bascom set out with a detachment to seek the Indians' trail. (Until recently, the raid was thought to have taken place the previous October, which, among other things, made the military's delay incomprehensible.)

The trail must have led to Apache Pass, for the next day Bascom set out for it with 54 infantrymen mounted on mules. They arrived on

3 February, finding 13 men there. Cochise was summoned.

He arrived the next day with several men, one of them his brother, also a woman and two

Above: *On the Trail of Geronimo* by Frederic Remington. Left: The body of Captain Crawford is brought to Lang's Ranch, near Cloverdale, New Mexico during the campaign to catch Geronimo. Below: General George Crook and two Apache scouts during the pursuit of Geronimo.

This photograph was taken after the capture of Geronimo (third from the left in the front row).

boys (some accounts state that the woman and one of the boys were his wife and son). Cochise and his men entered Bascom's tent, where Ward, who had come with Bascom, recognized him. Cochise denied having had any part in the raid and said that Coyotero Apache were responsible for it and were holding the boy prisoner. When Bascom said that he would intern Cochise's people until the boy was returned, the furious chief cut through the tent with his knife and dashed through the group of startled soldiers standing outside. They started shooting at him, but he escaped. The other Apache were held and the soldiers moved into the stone-walled stage station.

Cochise returned with a huge band the next day, including Francisco, the Coyotero chief, and many of his men. The two chiefs had often raided into Mexico together. A parley was arranged under white flags, with each leader accompanied by three unarmed men, but Bascom became suspicious before reaching the halfway point. Against Bascom's protests, three Overland Mail employees, Culver, Welch and Wallace, started forward to talk to the Apache and were seized. The white flags came down and the Bascom party made a dash to escape, Sergeant Smith being slightly wounded. Culver and Welch wrestled free of their captors and ran back under fire, both of them being wounded just before reaching safety, Welch fatally. Wallace was taken away by the Apache.

The stage came in ahead of schedule the next day, thus missing an ambush. Cochise now offered to exchange Wallace and 16 mules for Bascom's hostages, and the lieutenant agreed, if the stolen boy was produced. That evening a note from Wallace was delivered stating that the Apache had three more prisoners to trade the next day. That day started with the arrival of another stage which had been attacked on the way. A burned-out Mexican wagon and eight dead teamsters had been seen. Later in the day, Wallace was led out with a rope around his neck: Cochise would exchange him for the six Apache prisoners. Bascom, having established that the three other men were still captives, suggested a full exchange by both sides,

An Apache scout delivers the head of a hostile Apache to army officers.

but Cochise refused and Wallace was dragged away.

On the 8th, Apache attacked as some stock was being watered at the spring 800 yards from the station. After a rifle fight across the spring, the Apache ran off the whole herd, killing one stage employee and wounding two more. Indians were killed, too, possibly the first casualties suffered by the Chiricahua at the hands of Americans, and their deaths probably led to the killing and mutilation of Wallace and the three other captives. Twenty-five years of almost constant warfare had begun.

On the 10th, a handful of men led by Doctor B J D Irwin arrived bringing medical aid. They had run into Coyotero driving the stolen stock and captured three men, 13 cattle, and two horses, all being turned over to Bascom that evening. It was Irwin who found the mutilated hostages several days later. Meanwhile, 70 dragoons had arrived under Lieutenant I N Moore and, on their way back, they hanged the three Chiricahua and the three Coyotero. It was Irwin, not Bascom, who ordered the hangings. Indeed, Bascom protested. The Chiricahua woman and the two boys were later released. As for Bascom, he was killed a year later at the Battle of Valverde between Union and Confederate troops in New Mexico.

In April, the Overland Mail closed all its stations in the area. The Civil War broke out on 12 April. For some time, military operations in the Southwest had been at a virtual standstill because of the growing tension. Things were going the Apache's way. Fort Buchanan was at-tacked twice in June, and, in July, it and Fort Breckenridge were abandoned. On 1 August, Colonel Baylor declared Arizona to be Confederate territory and, during that month, the few remaining settlers in the area headed for Tucson. The town had been acquired by the United States as part of the Gadsden Purchase. Otherwise, except for a few isolated and strongly defended settlements, Arizona was cleared of whites.

On 28 February 1862, a Confederate force occupied Tucson, but by 20 May it was in the hands of Carleton and his California Volunteers. By now, Mangas Coloradas had almost wiped out the mining area of Piños Altos near the site of the Santa Rita massacre. Now he and Cochise laid an ambush for the Californians in Apache Pass. The two chiefs had some 500 warriors near the site of the 'Bascom Incident'. Into the west entrance of the pass came Captain Thomas L Roberts, a company of infantry, and a mountain howitzer battery. They were ahead of the wagon train, guarded by Captain Cremony and a company of cavalry. The troops badly needed water, but found themselves assailed by bullets and arrows from above. With his men strung out along the pass, Roberts was forced to order a retreat, but he was soon back with his howitzers. The Apache had never faced artillery before and had never imagined such powerful guns. They retreated, allowing the soldiers to reach the spring. But the Apache were not prepared to break off the action. Roberts secured his position at the spring and awaited the inevitable battle the next day, meanwhile sending a sergeant and five men back with a warning to Cremony and the wagon train.

Suddenly, Apache swept down on the party. Private John Teal was cut off from the rest and had to be abandoned. From behind his dead horse, he started shooting, bringing a huge warrior to the ground. It was Mangas Coloradas, and the fighting stopped. The amazed Teal walked to Cremony's camp not knowing what he had achieved. Meanwhile, the chief was carried in a sling and taken to a Mexican village, where it was made clear to a doctor by grimfaced Mimbreño braves that if their leader died, the town died also. Helped no doubt by Mangas's iron strength, the doctor succeeded in curing his patient and, after convalescing, the chief was back with his people in the Mimbres Mountains.

Back at Apache Pass, no one knew anything of this high drama and Roberts, complete with artillery, had an easy passage the next morning. Carleton ordered that a fort be built to protect the spring and Fort Bowie was erected.

Mangas Coloradas had not long to live. He was about 70 years old and seemed to have felt that the time had come to try and make peace with the 'Anglos', the peace he had once enjoyed for a brief time with them. In January 1863, he was camped near the abandoned Piños Altas mining settlement, little knowing that Carleton and his Californians, and many others, wanted all the Apache dead by any means. One group that was after the chief was the 40-strong gold-seeking Walker party from California, led by the ex-mountain man, Joseph Reddeford Walker. If they could capture Mangas and use him as a hostage, life would be simpler. They were joined by Captain Edmund D Shirland, First Cavalry, and some California Volunteers, whose commander, General West, was less interested in hostages than in dead men.

Though the sequence of events is disputed, the outlines are clear enough. Despite the misgivings of his warriors, Mangas, wanting to talk peace, allowed himself to be lured into Shirland's camp on his own under the safety of a white flag and was promptly captured. He was hurried to the abandoned Fort McLane, where General Joseph E West, so Private Stocking of the California Volunteers later recalled, told the guards: 'I want him dead or alive tomorrow morning, do you understand? I want him dead.'

There is no reason to doubt the story. One of the miners, Daniel Conner, related the rest of it. On sentry duty, he found himself near Mangas and his two guards. He noticed that they were annoying the old chief, though they stopped when they saw him. So Conner watched what was going on from a distance. It was a very cold night and the men had a log fire. The guards were heating their bayonets in the fire and putting them against Mangas's feet and legs. Finally, the chief told them in Spanish that he was not a child to be played with, and they shot him. Naturally, it was reported that he had been killed attempting to escape.

He was scalped and his head was cut off, and boiled so that the skull could be sold to a phrenologist. Carleton put out a statement proclaiming the wickedness of the late chief and stating that he had been killed. Later, West, accused of brutality in the affair, gave a totally false account of it—Mangas had allegedly taken on no less than seven soldiers—and got away with his crime.

The death of Mangas Coloradas made Cochise more implacable than ever, while Geronimo and Victorio, respectively Mimbres and Warm Springs Apache and destined to become famous, must have burned to avenge him. The latter was to call the murder 'perhaps the greatest wrong ever done to the Indians.'

It is impossible to chart the exploits of more than a handful of the campaigns the Apache waged. The Mescalero's behavior was typical of the Apache will to fight for survival. Hunted down by Carleton, who made Kit Carson leader of the campaign against them, they were driven to the Bosque Redondo where they were to be the uneasy neighbors of the Navaho. They did their considerable best to settle there as farmers, but the arrival of the Navaho made their position hopeless. There were too many Indians for the size of the reservation, even if the tribes had been friendly, which they were not. So in 1865, some 500 of the Mescalero left the reservation and raided eastern New Mexico and western Texas, also cutting deep into Mexico. In 1871, most of them settled on the Fort Stanton Reservation, but were soon being persecuted by local settlers. In 1874, there were killings by a white mob and the Indians fled—only to be attacked by troops who were meant to bring them back peacefully. Later, Victorio settled with them and, as we shall see, some Mescalero broke out with him in 1879.

Cochise's conflict with the whites after Mangas Coloradas's death lasted almost a decade. Carleton and his Californians were replaced by Regulars after the Civil War ended in 1865, the impossibility of their task being reflected in General Sherman's wry comment: 'We had one war with Mexico to take Arizona, and we should have another one to make her take it back.'

Victorio and Nana, Warm Springs Apache, attended a peace conference in 1865, heard that they were destined for the hated Bosque Redondo, asked for time to think it over, and disappeared with their bands. The guerrilla war that followed made it suicidal for whites to take risks, and, as the decade wore on, raiding became more widespread than ever.

There were more whites to kill. Arizona became a territory in 1863, and, by 1870, despite the constant warfare, settlers, miners and ranchers had pushed the population up by another 10,000. There is evidence that Cochise longed for peace, for the Apache's numbers decreased as the steady flood of whites flowed into the territory.

In February, 1871, however, an event occurred that made peace impossible. In charge of a small post north of Cochise's stronghold was an idealistic young New Englander, Lieutenant Royal Whitman. To the post, known as Camp Grant, came Chief Eskiminzin of the Aravaipa Apache, who, so he said, wanted to settle down peacefully. He was tired of fighting and of being harassed. Just how warlike he and his people had been is not certain, reports differ, but Whitman believed in him. He agreed to let the Indians stay near the fort and they agreed to hand in their firearms. There were 500 of them and they set up a thriving community, which included a few Apache from other bands. Some worked happily for local ranchers.

Raids continued elsewhere and there were accusations that they had been carried out by Eskiminzin's men. The accusations came from Indian-haters in Tucson and those who were perhaps waxing fat thanks to army contracts. Peaceful Apache would ruin them.

An expedition was organized by a lawyer and ex-Indian fighter named Oury, which finally consisted of six Anglos, 42 Mexicans, and 92 Apache-hating Papago Indians. Whitman heard about the expedition too late.

The attack lasted less than half an hour, and after the slaughter, the rapes, and the mutilation, the murderous gang fled. They had killed a disputed number, possibly something near the 125 that Whitman claimed had died. Nearly 30 Apache children were carried away to slavery in Mexico, and of the known dead a mere eight were men.

The massacre, Westerners apart, stunned the entire nation from President Grant downwards. It made a mockery of his Peace Policy and he threatened martial law if the culprits were not tried. They were and, frontier fashion, they were all acquitted. Whitman did what he could for the surviving Indians, but a vicious campaign, based on his belief in the Apache, destroyed his career. Ironically, the one good thing about the trial was that it showed the flimsy nature of the evidence against the Apache.

In June, General Crook, veteran of Indian wars in the Northwest, arrived to assume the command of the Department of Arizona. Also arriving in the Southwest was the humanitarian, Vincent Colyer, representing the Indian Bureau. President Grant wanted peace in the area. The policy of extermination was not only vile, it was a failure.

Colyer met Eskiminzin, whose tribulations were not yet over. He also hoped to meet Delchay, chief of the Tonto, but that warrior's experience of the Bluecoats had been so unfortunate when he had been at peace that he missed the chance to meet the sympathetic Colyer. Crook, who was as honest as he was tough, and was finally to become one of the greatest champions of the Apache, had little time for the well-meaning Colyer. He would soon be letting the hostiles know his feelings via spies and captive Indians, and was to organize Apache to track down Apache. His intentions were simple. Any band away from the reservation was to be considered hostile. His men, white or Apache, were to allow those Indians wishing to surrender to do so. The rest would be hunted down, captured or killed, but women and children would not be harmed. His troops must keep on and on. This was to mean on foot, as horses simply could not cope with some of the roughest terrain on the continent.

Crook was not pleased when the pious General Howard arrived, sent by Grant. Howard, who had fought the Nez Percé, was liable to drop to his knees at key moments. Yet it was the one-armed Howard who made peace with Cochise.

He could never have done it without the remarkable frontiersman, Tom Jeffords, whose blood brotherhood with Cochise is one of the classic stories of the West.

Jeffords had come to Arizona in 1862 as an army scout. Later, with a contract to organize the mail between Tucson and Fort Bowie, he and his riders were ambushed so many times that he took action in a way that might have been his death sentence. Alone, the tall red-bearded frontiersman went to see Cochise in his stronghold and asked the amazed but impressed chief to allow him and his men to carry their mail in safety. He got what he wanted and, more important, each man gained a friend and a friendship of depth that was to last until Cochise died in 1874. Jeffords lived on until 1914. However, apart from this strange oasis of peace based on deep feeling and mutual respect, the war went on.

Before Howard's meeting, thanks to Jeffords, another army officer had tried to make peace with him. He was General Gordon Granger, and Cochise, weary of war and the steady de-

Victorio, chief of the Mimbreno Apaches, killed in 1880.

struction of his people, agreed to meet him. As the whites wanted to move him to the hated Tularosa reservation, despite a promise by Granger, war flared up again, but from the meeting, conducted in Spanish, came a description of Cochise by Dr A N Ellis:

While he was talking we had a fine opportunity to study this most remarkable man. Evidently he was about fifty-eight years of age, although he looked very much younger; his height, five feet, ten inches; in person lithe and wiry, every muscle being well rounded and firm. A silver thread was now and then visible in his otherwise black hair, which he wore cut straight around his head about on a level with his chin. His countenance displayed great force.

Ellis wrote Cochise's speech down. It included the following:

When I was young I walked all over this country, east and west, and saw no other people than the Apaches. After many summers I walked again and found another race of people who had come to take it. How is it? Why is it that the Apaches want to die—that they carry their lives on their finger nails? They roam over the hills and plains and want the heavens to fall on them. The Apaches were once a great nation; they are now but a few . . . Tell me, if the Virgin Mary has walked throughout all the land, why has she never entered the lodge of the Apache?

Things were very different for Howard, who could speak for President Grant. For all his actions against the Nez Percé Howard was a true Christian and a humane man. Taken by Jeffords to Cochise, he made a deep impression on him and gave him, after much discussion, what he wanted, a reservation in the Chiricahuas and a valley beyond. But Cochise insisted on one other thing, Jeffords as the Indians' agent. Only too well aware of the difficulties in store, and knowing the low pay, Jeffords nevertheless finally agreed. He could not let Cochise and his people down.

When the great Chiricahua died, his sons, Taza and Naiche (Nachez) persuaded Jeffords to remain. With Cochise gone, however, his position became steadily more impossible. It was too easy now without Cochise's influence for renegades to use the reservation, for some Chiricahua to resume raids on Mexico, and to

Chato, a chief of the Chiricahua tribe of Apaches.

Eskiminizin, the head chief of the Pinal-Coyotero.

take up with the nonreservation bands. To make things worse, the government cut the supply of beef to the reservation. Finally, after Jeffords, with troops, failed to dislodge some renegades in the Dragoon Mountains, the Chiricahua, to the joy of Indian-haters, were told they must leave their beloved home for the San Carlos reservation, which already contained 4000 Apache. Taza, who tried to hold his people together, died on an official trip to Washington; Jeffords was eased out of his post; the Chiricahua were moved to a place they disliked which contained Apache hostile to them.

In fact only 325 Chiricahua went to San Carlos. The authorities tried to make out that the majority went, but Jeffords reckoned that 140 went to Warm Springs and some 400 were at large. This figure was challenged by General Kautz, who had succeeded Crook (now fighting the Sioux), and who accused Jeffords of adding to the figures to stop charges of fraud being brought against him for the number of Indians he stated he had fed! Geronimo and Taza's family were among those who crossed into Mexico.

The vast San Carlos reservation was part of the new policy of concentrating Indians in Indian Territory or large areas elsewhere, normally those not yet wanted by whites.

The new agent at San Carlos was John Clum, who arrived there in 1874, aged 22. He was so sure of himself that he believed that he could handle San Carlos on his own if only the army would let him alone. For all his arrogance, he was honest, brave and bright. Anyone else would have despaired of San Carlos, not least because so many Indians hostile to each other were there. Clum never despaired. It was Clum who brought the Chiricahua to San Carlos, Clum who, with the help of his Apache police, caught Geronimo at the Warm Springs reservation after he had slipped back across the border, and Clum who brought Victorio and 343 of his people to San Carlos from Warm Springs after the closing of that reservation had been ordered. The closing should never have happened, but that was not Clum's business. Finally, he boasted that he could handle all the Apache in Arizona! Being turned down, he resigned in 1877 and, later, became the editor of the celebrated Tombstone *Epitaph*.

Without Clum, the situation at San Carlos deteriorated. It was always an unhealthy place for those Indians used to the mountains, and now it was badly and, in some cases, corruptly run. Food supplies were not getting through and miners were invading the reservation. In

September 1877, Victorio broke out with 310 Apache, heading for Ojo Caliente. The breakaway failed and they were held for a year at Ojo Caliente while the Indian Bureau brooded, then decided to send them back to San Carlos. Victorio took off once again, this time with 80 men, the rest of his people being sent to hated San Carlos. Wanting to settle down, he first tried to stop at Ojo Caliente early in 1879, then seemed to find a home, and a welcome from the agent, at Tularosa with the Mescalero. The agent promised to try and bring his people's families there, but in September, fearing arrest for an old crime, Victorio fled to Mexico. From his base there he went on a savage, brilliant series of raids with his own followers, plus some Mescalero and Chiricahua. Both sides of the border were in a state of terror until, in 1880, he was trapped and killed in Mexico. Thanks to gross mismanagement, he had been driven on to a wild and terrible course until an Indian scout with the Mexican army killed him.

In mid-1881, it was Nana's turn. Seventy or so years old, this Warm Springs veteran, at first with 15, then 40, men (when some Mescalero joined him) went on a six-week raid, killing over 30 people and eluding 1000 troops and hundreds of civilians. Then he escaped to Mexico. 1881 also saw an outbreak among the White Mountain Apache in the forests and mountains to the north of the San Carlos reservation. A medicine man, Noch-ay-del-klinne, had predicted the return of dead chiefs and the driving out of the whites. The excitement stirred even the loyal White Mountains scouts at Fort Apache. In August, agent J C Tiffany, sent Colonel Eugene Carr and 85 cavalrymen, plus 23 scouts, to the medicine man's village at Cibicu Creek. A fight broke out in which the scouts mutinied, but though the medicine man was killed and the revolt was put down, it resulted in general unrest at San Carlos and an outbreak on 30 September of 74 Chiricahua under Naiche, Juh, Geronimo and Chato, who later joined up with Nana and the remnants of Victorio's band.

In 1882, the most sensational event was Loco's raid. Not that it started as his. Chato, Naiche and Chihuahua, possibly also Geronimo, set off northward and headed for San Carlos, cutting telegraph wires and, among other feats, killing Chief of Police Sterling and, according to some accounts, playing football with his head. They proceeded to urge a renowned warrior named Loco to renounce the path of peace; they pointed a gun at him! He and many other Chiricahua and Warm Springs Indians fled with the visitors so determined to free them.

Among the troops after them was Colonel Forsyth, who, with 50 frontiersmen, had gained such fame against the Sioux and Cheyenne at the Arikaree River in 1868. He and his men were just in time to save one of his detachments, which had been ambushed in a canyon. The Apache were greatly outnumbered, but fought such a fine rear-guard action that nearly all the band got across the border.

There disaster struck. Colonel Lorenzo Garcia of the Sixth Mexican Infantry ambushed the Apache, killing many of their women and children. The leaders all escaped. As a result of the outbreak, more and more troops poured into Arizona, and in September 1882, Crook returned from his service against the Sioux.

The previous July, Mexico and the United States had signed a vital treaty that allowed their respective soldiers to cross the border in pursuit of hostiles. Despite this, the Apache were by no means finished.

The events, some of them controversial, that followed his coming leave no doubt of Crook's greatness as a leader and a human being. He was amazed at the forebearance of the reservation Apache. He talked to individual Indians and found that agents and others had robbed them of their rations, and that whites had tried to stir up the Apache so as to get them driven off their land. Miners and squatters were now ejected and the bands allowed to live where they wanted to on the vast reservation. Soldiers were barred unless needed. Meanwhile, a grand jury railed against the officials who had so ill-served the reservation 'which is a disgrace to the civilization of the age and a foul blot upon the national escutcheon. We feel it our duty . . . to express our utter abhorrence of the conduct of Agent Tiffany and that class of reverend pecculators who have cursed Arizona as Indian officials . . .' It is uncertain if Tiffany himself was quite as bad as this, but the charges are all too typical of the average officials under whom the Indians suffered.

In March 1883, a raid on a mining camp near Tombstone gave Crook his chance to cross into Mexico. His scouts found the Chiricahua camp in the Sierra Madres, and in April he set out with 193 Apaches, 45 cavalrymen and two pack trains.

Because he was the last major leader of the Apache—who themselves regarded Naiche as their hereditary chief—and because his campaigns occurred when the main wars were over, Geronimo's importance has been overrated. This started in his own time when the booming newspaper business needed exciting copy. The build-up has been ever greater in our time, when he has become one of the key figures in the Indian Pantheon. Yet for all the exaggeration, he was a remarkable man. A Mimbreño, whose grandfather had been chief of the Nednhi Apache, he started as one of Mangas Coloradas's young braves. He was scarred emotionally for life when he lost his wife and three young children in a massacre organized by General Carasco, a savage Mexican dictator, who was later poisoned by his own countrymen. His name was Goyathlay (He Who Yawns), but in a battle with Mexicans one of them called him Geronimo (Jerome in Spanish) and it stuck. He was a medicine man, not a chief, though he was a leader, partly because Naiche, Cochise's son, had no great ambitions to be a chief in the fullest sense of the word. Handsome and elegant and liking the ladies, he was, for an Apache, easygoing.

Geronimo became one of Cochise's men, and, later, he was one of those who slipped regularly across the border. With the move to San Carlos in 1876, he and other irreconcilables based themselves in northern Mexico. On a visit to relatives at the Warm Springs reservation, he found himself face to face with Clum. Surrounded by too many Indian police to fight, he was taken to San Carlos. He decamped in 1878, came back in December 1879, but was one of those who vanished again at the time of the Noch-ay-del-klinne incident. A vivid description of him by Charles F. Lummis, fleshes out the many photographs of him:

He was a compactly built, dark-faced man of one hundred and seventy pounds, and about five feet, eight inches in height. The man who once saw his face will never forget it. Cruel-ler features were never cut. The nose was broad and heavy, the forehead low and wrinkled, the chin full and strong, the eyes like two bits of obsidian with a light behind them. The mouth was a most noticeable feature—a sharp, straight, thin-lipped gash of generous length and without one softening curve.

Captain Emmett Crawford led the scouts on the 1883 campaign. He was a brilliant officer and his scouts were all Crook could have hoped for. Apart from the freedom of choice they had as Indians and Apache, scouting made a welcome change from reservation life, especially for those who were not Chiricahua. Crawford and his men took a hostile camp by surprise, killing nine and taking five prisoner. The Chiricahua wanted peace, and started to come in on 17 May. On the 20th, Geronimo arrived. Three tense meetings took place, at the third of which chief of scouts Al Seiber is said to have sat with a revolver under his shirt in case of treachery. There was none. Loco and Nana came in, too. Geronimo asked if Crook could stay while he and Naiche gathered up their scattered bands, including women and children. Crook replied that his supplies were low and that he could stay only while operations were in progress, but he got Geronimo's promise to return to the reservation. He could hardly arrest him without the rest vanishing. Few believed that Geronimo would keep his promise.

By 29 May, 374 Apaches had come in. The next day Crook started north with most of them, San Carlos being reached in June. There followed a hiatus and Lieutenant Britton Davis (who was later to write the classic *The Truth about Geronimo*) was sent to the border to await the rest. Crook's gamble seemed to have failed, but on 20 December a small group appeared and, on 7 February 1884, Chato and 19 more arrived, followed later in the month by Geronimo. The 350 head of stolen cattle he brought with him had to be returned, to his annoyance!

Crook had triumphed, though the corrupt gang who wanted no peace did their best to smear him with rumors that, in fact, it was Geronimo who had captured him.

He was now able to state that 'for the first time in the history of that people, every member of the Apache tribe is at peace.' Crook was

Old Nana, a famous Apache chief.

determined that it should stay that way. Britton Davis was given the toughest assignment—to guard Geronimo, Chato and other leaders—at Turkey Creek near Fort Apache. Few young officers on the frontier ever had more responsibility thrust on them and took it with such grace under pressure. He depended on two scouts in particular, Chato and a tough but utterly loyal Apache called Dutchy—because he looked German. Davis's life was saved by them when the very dangerous Ka-ya-ten-nae tried to ambush him. The warrior ended up in Alcatraz, then a military prison, but was brought back by Crook to become, despite his nature, a fine scout.

Yet inevitably perhaps, a breakout occurred, through no fault of Davis's. Restless, bored, forbidden to brew their beer, tiswin, fearing rumors of impending arrest, a group of Apache told Davis that they had been drunk the night before and what did he intend doing about it? Playing for time, Davis said he would contact Crook: there were too many potential hostiles to arrest. He sent an urgent telegram to San Carlos, where a newcomer, Captain Pierce, showed it to Seiber for his advice. Seiber, usually utterly reliable, had a hangover and brushed the message aside, saying the incident was no more than a tiswin drunk, and Pierce pigeonholed the message with disastrous results. It was months before Crook saw it.

If Crook had received the message, the outbreak that followed would either never have occurred or it would have been rapidly contained. As it was, Geronimo, Mangus, who was Magnas Coloradas's son, Naiche, Chihuahua and old Nana left, the total number of fugitives being 24 men, eight boys old enough to be war-

riors, and 92 women and children.

The Apache were soon at odds with each other, Chihuahua being bitter that Geronimo had told them that both Chato and Britton Davis were dead and that they would soon be arrested by the troops. After angry exchanges, they split up, Naiche hoping to return to Fort Apache. After a fight with Davis and his scouts, however, Chihuahua fled to Mexico.

Geronimo and Naiche were there already. Meanwhile, Crook had every waterhole on the border guarded, as he expected the hostiles to return north for ammunition. Crawford was now in Mexico with his scouts, soon followed by Captain Wirt Davis and scouts under Lieutenant Gatewood. Next into Mexico was Davis, who joined Crawford, then acted separately again. The going was so tough and his command grew so ragged that he had trouble convincing Mexican troops that he was an officer. Their leader wanted to shoot his entire command. After a 500-mile march and all his previous adventures, he decided to resign his commission, and became the manager of a ranch and its mines in Chihuahua. Meanwhile, Crawford ended an arduous campaign back at Fort Apache, as the enlistment period of his scouts was almost over.

In November, Chihuahua's brother Ulzana, with just a dozen men, carried out a daring raid in the Nana tradition. In four weeks, and covering 1200 miles, the raiders started by killing all the Apache they could find on the Fort Apache reservation. They aimed especially at scouts and their families. They attacked a ranch, ambushed a cavalry troop, stealing horses all the while, and returned to Mexico having killed at least 38. They had lost one man.

Now Sheridan was at Fort Bowie promoting Washington's belief that all Chiricahua and Warm Springs Indians must be moved from the Southwest. Sheridan believed on principle that the use of Apache scouts was wrong.

In December, Captain Crawford led his devoted scouts into Mexico, and in January surprised Geronimo's camp, capturing horses and supplies. Geronimo decided to negotiate, probably because Chiricahua were now acting as scouts. Then an appalling tragedy occurred. Mexican irregulars suddenly appeared and started firing, thinking these scouts were hostiles. Crawford, with Maus and Tom Horn in charge of the scouts, tried to stop the firing, but after it had ceased, a sudden shot (a volley according to Maus) rang out and Crawford was mortally wounded. Horn was also wounded, along with four more men. The enraged scouts killed the Mexican commander and several others. The next day, Maus, who was sure that the Mexicans knew they were facing Americans, went to their camp, only to be detained until he had given them mules.

Geronimo, who had watched the entire episode, told Maus he would meet Crook at the border in 'two moons' time. Maus then headed north, bringing several warriors with him, including Nana, and the families of Geronimo and Naiche. The Indians arrived at Crook's camp on 25 March 1886, Crook reckoning that he would have needed 1000 men to capture them if they had been unwilling to talk. He did his best to sow dissension in the Apache camp by sending in the now reformed Kay-at-en-ae among them. On the 27th, Chihuahua sent word he was on his way, but Geronimo and Nana came as well. They said that they would surrender only if it was promised that they would be returned to the reservation after the two years' exile in the East which Crook told them was their inevitable punishment. Crook agreed. It made more sense than more war.

Sheridan, after speaking to President Cleveland, overruled Crook, and demanded unconditional surrender, but the dispute was now irrelevant. Geronimo had vanished again. Crook had telegraphed Sheridan from Fort Bowie, assuming that the Chiricahua would be proceeding there with the scouts. But just before they had reached the border, an American bootlegger named Tribolet sold the Indians liquor, got them drunk, scared them with tales of what would happen to them; the last Apache war had started.

On the Apache side were Geronimo, Naiche, 16 warriors, 13 women, and six children. Crook, on informing Sheridan, was reprimanded so severely (his scouts were accused of disloyalty) that he felt impelled to resign. General Nelson A Miles arrived at Fort Bowie on 12 April, while those Apache who had surrendered were sent to Fort Marion, Florida. Miles had some 5000 troops under him. Having no great opinion of Crook's Apache scouts, quaintly believing that white soldiers were better at tracking down Apache, he decided that cavalry could track down Geronimo. True, he had a very tough cavalry leader in Captain Lawton, but inevitably the cavalrymen were soon dismounted because of the rough terrain.

Miles had 30 heliograph stations built, which flashed messages on both sides of the border. This was a plus, but guarding every waterhole, spring, and pass proved impossible. Miles was forced to use Apache scouts, who proved invaluable.

Finally, Miles was forced to use not just the scouts already in action, but a warrior named Kieta who had deserted Geronimo. He told Miles that if a handful of men known to Geronimo got through to him, they might talk him into surrendering. So he, another Apache called Martine, and Lieutenant Gatewood (the only one of Crook's key young officers with the new command) set out to find Geronimo.

He proved to be in the Torres Mountains south of the Arizona-New Mexico border. The two scouts went in. Geronimo kept Kieta as a hostage, Martine carrying a message asking why Gatewood had not come himself. However, Naiche, the true leader, sent word that the party would be safe. By sheer luck, Lawton and his command arrived at this moment. He, not Gatewood, was to get the credit for finding Geronimo. Gatewood, after all, was a Crook protégé!

Gatewood went in alone. He gave Geronimo Miles's message: 'Surrender and you will be sent to Florida with your families, there to await the President's decision as to your final disposition.' Otherwise they would be fought to the bitter end. He told the Apache that all their friends and relatives were already in Florida. Back on the reservation they would be among enemies.

The next day Geronimo agreed to surrender, asking for protection against Mexican attack on the journey. They started north on 25 August. The end came at Skeleton Canyon just across the Arizona border, though Miles delayed his appearance for several days, arriving on 3 September. Mangus and a few others were still at large, to be rounded up later, but the Apache Wars ended at Skeleton Canyon.

The aftermath was cruel and disgraceful. True, the situation was complicated. There were those in the Southwest who wanted to get the Apache into court, try them and hang them, while the population of Arizona as a whole wanted the Chiricahua banished forever. Miles had earlier built up Apache hopes of getting a reservation in the West. On 7 September, the government decided that the Geronimo band should be imprisoned subject to trial, but on the 8th, to the strains of *Auld Lang Syne*, they were put aboard a train bound for Florida. It was to be some time before they got there because of fierce arguments about what should be done and what had been promised, but at least Miles helped spare them a trial in the West. Indeed, if that had been the end of the story, Miles's part in it would have not been unworthy, despite his refusal to give credit to Gatewood. As it was, his treatment of the Chiricahua was abominable. Martine and Kieta were sent to Florida, so were 381 Chirichua and Warm Springs Apache, including Crook's loyal scouts, and even Crook's noted scout, Dutchy. So were 13 Apaches who had been taken as a delegation to Washington, including Chato. On their way back they were detained in Kansas, then found themselves in Florida with the rest. Finally, there were 509 there.

There would have been one more, but, as if to demonstrate that an Apache could never be beaten, one warrior, Massai, managed to escape from the prison train bearing him into exile just before it reached St. Louis. He made his way back to Arizona and lived for many years as a noted 'Broncho' Apache, until finally he was killed. Al Seiber was one of many who tried without success to capture him.

In Florida, whose climate was so unsuitable for them, the Apache death rate was high. Their children were sent to the Carlyle Indian School in Pennsylvania, where 50 of them died. Other Apache besides the Chiricahua and the Warm Springs people found themselves sent East. Eskiminzin, who had yet again been trying to live in peace, was accused of being in contact with the Apache Kid, an outlaw ex-scout whose treatment at the hands of the whites had driven him to crime. With 40 Araviapa, Eskiminzin was sent to Mount Vernon Barracks, Alabama.

Geronimo and the men of his final band were sent to Fort Pickens, to be joined by Mangus and others. The rest went to Fort Marion, where at least there was a humane officer in charge. Later, all were to be at Fort Marion, then at Mount Vernon Barracks, Alabama.

The Apache had some champions, most notably, General Crook. He visited them in 1890 just before his death and was very warmly received. Other friends included John Clum. With their aid and growing public support, the Apache were sent to Fort Sill, Oklahoma, in 1894, which was at least a more suitable climate for them and it was in the West. There they had a sympathetic guardian in Lieutenant Hugh Scott. However, only Eskiminzin and his band ever got back to Arizona. In 1913, the rest had a choice of staying in Oklahoma or joining the Mescalero on their reservation. Two thirds went there.

Geronimo was exhibited from time to time at expositions, but his greatest moment came when he rode in President Theodore Roosevelt's Inaugural Procession in 1901. The army chiefs were furious that the old 'killer' was to be on parade, but the West-loving President wanted, as he said, 'to give the people a good show.' There were other Indians there that day, including Quanah Parker, but Geronimo stole the show, his reception being second only to that of the President. He asked Roosevelt later if he and his people could return to Arizona, but was told the truth—that Arizona would not have the Chiricahua back. He died at Fort Sill in 1909.

Muchacho Negro, a chief of the Mescalero Apache.

6
THE ROAD
FROM
WOUNDED KNEE

In 1877, the year Sitting Bull crossed the border into Canada, the North-West Mounted Police found themselves coping with some 4000 Sioux. They did so firmly but fairly and Sitting Bull struck up a friendship with Major James Walsh, into whose area of Saskatchewan the Sioux had flooded.

Yet it became the Mounties' job to get the Indians out. There were not enough buffalo left to feed the Canadian Blackfeet and the Cree. Famine might lead to raids across the border and back, and there was always the danger of intertribal war; the Blackfeet were not well disposed towards the Sioux. Finally, they went south, Sitting Bull leading his hungry band to Fort Burford, Montana, in 1881.

These were grim days for the Sioux and most other Indians. The policy was to make them into white people. Those who responded positively were 'progressives,' the rest were 'non-progressives'. To be a farmer and a Christian was the ideal of well-meaning whites. The new agent at the Standing Rock Reservation, to which Sitting Bull was sent after two years' imprisonment, was one such. He was James McLaughlin, whose wife was of Sioux descent. He tried to break the hold Sitting Bull had over his people by appointing other chiefs in his place, but Sitting Bull remained the heart and soul of the nonprogressives.

This was a time when well-meaning whites and also land-grabbers were propagating the same disastrous doctrine of individual ownership of land by Indians. Well-wishers failed to

Left: Chief Sitting Bull (1834-1890). Above: A photograph taken of Sitting Bull and 'Buffalo Bill' Cody while the chief was touring with Cody's show. Below: Sitting Bull's son, Crow Foot.

Top: The death of
Sitting Bull. Inset: Red
Tomahawk, the Indian
policeman who killed
him. Left: Wovoka or The
Cutter, also known as
Jack Wilson. He was the Paiute 'Messiah', son of
Tavibo, the prophet. Below left: The ghost shirt of
the Arapahoe. Bottom: Hypnotized performers in a
ghost dance.

A Navajo Indian of Gallup, New Mexico. He is wearing the traditional native costume with necklace and silver belt.

see that the only real power the Indian had was his tribe, while those after his land realized that their chance had come. Despite a vocal white minority's objections, the Dawes Act was passed in 1887.

Named for Senator Henry Dawes, it not only advocated the division of reservations into individual allotments, but opened many millions of acres of reservation lands to whites.

As far as the Sioux were concerned, their great reservation was to be made into six small ones with nine million acres up for grabs.

It was now that the last Indian messiah appeared, a Nevada Paiute named Wovoka. His message was peaceful enough. He taught his followers a simple shuffling dance and spoke of a new world where Indians would be free of whites and be reunited in bliss with their dead. Most Indians accepted it as a peaceful doctrine, but not the despairing Sioux. They came to believe that Wovoka's message meant war and that by wearing ghost shirts white men's bullets could not touch them.

Hunger and disease made the Sioux more desperate, and it became clear to the military that war was a possibility. But, with so many forts now surrounding the Sioux, it would be a very one-sided war. The Pine Ridge reservation was the most turbulent, partly because a weak agent had demanded troops. Six hundred arrived at the Pine Ridge and Rosebud agencies, some Indians gathering at them to avoid trouble, others heading to far corners of the reservations to continue ghost dancing.

Miles now ordered the arrest of Sitting Bull and the Minneconjou chief Big Foot. McLaughlin, who had wanted to net Sitting Bull for some weeks, sent Indian police to his tent at dawn on 15 December 1890, backed up at a distance by troops. The great chief was seized. His enraged followers attacked his captors, and in the ensuing scrimmage, Sergeant Red Tomahawk shot Sitting Bull dead. 'Indians!' Sitting Bull had once shouted in his despair as the Sioux Reservation was signed away by other chiefs and broken up. 'There are no Indians left but me!'

Big Foot, a noted peacemaker, was in the Badlands of Dakota with some 350 men, women, and children. He had fled when troops had approached his band, but he was now on his way to the Pine Ridge Agency, when he was intercepted by four troops of the Seventh Cavalry on 28 December. On the 29th, Colonel Forsyth (not the hero of Beecher's Island) surrounded the Indians with 500 men and placed four Hotchkiss rapid-firing guns to cover them. Big Foot lay in his tent with pneumonia. There was snow in the air.

Forsyth decided that the Sioux must be disarmed. The atmosphere was tense, for the Indians had heard rumors of being sent to Florida, while many of the Seventh's men were raw

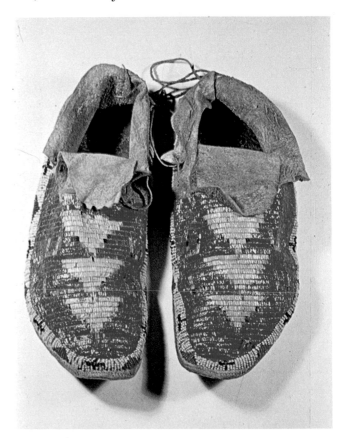

A pair of quill-work moccasins of the Cheyenne.

recruits. Only a few rifles were given up and the troops were brought in closer until the warriors were hemmed into a hollow square. Other troops were sent to search the women for weapons.

At this electric moment, a medicine man named Yellow Bird began dancing, shouting that the Sioux's ghost shirts would keep out white men's bullets. A scuffle started as a soldier searched an Indian, then a shot rang out. Yellow Bird threw some dust into the air,

The fight at Wounded Knee, South Dakota.

whereupon several braves threw aside their blankets, then raised their rifles.

The soldiers opened fire and in the confusion, noise, dust and smoke, the last round of the Indians Wars began. Half of Big Foot's band were killed at the first blast of fire, with the Indians and soldiers almost face-to-face. The survivors fought ferociously, those without guns using clubs and knives. Women joined them from the tents with their children, many of them taking part in the fight.

It was bound to be more of a massacre than a battle. The Indians who survived retreated to a deep ravine, the Hotchkiss guns raining shells down on them as they sang their death songs. It was soon over and the bloody ground was covered with a blanket of snow. More than 150 men, women and children died and 50 were wounded compared to 23 dead soldiers. The massacre was a tragic accident, not planned slaughter, as some have tried to claim, but the result was the same. For the last time, strong medicine—on this horrifying occasion the ghost shirts—had failed.

In theory, the Dawes Act was geared to teach the Indians to stand on their own feet. In fact, its policy of detribalization was disastrous. It aimed to Americanize the Indians. Later, even the men's long hair was banned, forcibly if necessary. The Dawes Act sounded good on paper—160 acres to heads of families, smaller spreads to other Indians—but it resulted in one of history's most successful land grabs. From 1887–1934, some 86 million acres out of 138 million were stolen from the Indians.

A determined attack was made on the Indians' religions. Those children taken to special schools, were taught to despise their past by well-meaning teachers. In fact, the Indians only hope of survival as Indians lay in the *tribe*, as it does for those who wish it today. True, individual Indians have risen to the top in many walks of life, but the majority still strive to keep as much of the old life as is possible. It may be awkward and baffling for the rest of the nation, because most of the old life is gone beyond recall for most Indians, but it is their right to try.

Proof of the fraudulent nature of the Dawes Act was that the Indians of the Southwest were relatively untouched by it. Few wanted what was left of their land. Elsewhere, land sharks went to extreme lengths, becoming 'friends' of Indians, guardians of their children and beneficiaries of their wills. Some could not wait, judging by unusually high murder rates in some areas.

Of course, some Indians, who acquired the whites' love of property, prospered in the white world, as did those suddenly oil-rich Indians who managed to hold on to their gains. Other Indians remained as army scouts, still more working in circuses, most notably with that good friend of Indians (whatever he had done earlier to their buffalo), Buffalo Bill Cody. As a result, a few Indians got to know London and even the delights of Venetian gondolas thanks to him. They were a tiny minority. Most officials, coping with the majority, simply could not understand that Indians might be better off as part of a tribe, or that so many of the tribes were so very different from each other.

At least World War I helped the Indians. Veterans got the vote as a result of it, all Indians on reservations getting it in 1924, though Arizona and New Mexico banned off-reservation and illiterate Indians from voting until 1959.

By the 1920s, the situation of the Indians was worse than ever. Efforts at turning them into farmers had mostly failed, not least because of the nature of many reservations. Not until 1930 did the death rate start to decline, while some Indians were so suspicious of whites that they would not use the improved medical facilities that were gradually introduced.

Then came the Depression and hope, in the shape of Roosevelt's New Deal. Already some whites had realized that the tribal system must be preserved. Now, in 1934, the Wheeler-Howard Act reversed the Dawes Act. It was not as easy as that. Space does not permit a long account, but the fact is that the majority of Indians, whose past is now so much better understood, are still in a wretched position in the white world. True, there are striking successes, notably the excellence of the San Carlos Apache cattle business and the Iroquois construction workers who specialize in skyscrapers. Some suggest that this is not just an aptitude for the work and a lack of fear of heights, but the challenge involved.

The majority, however, are as depressed as ever and prey to alcoholism and disease. The

dangerous 1950s are gone when under the guise of good will, reservations were threatened with closing. One tribe, the timber-rich Menominee of Wisconsin, actually had their reservation closed with disastrous results, but in 1973, the decision was reversed. Now, with lawyers winning claims for lands fraudulently taken from the Indians, vast sums of money are being won by some tribes, but the exploitation of the West for mineral wealth continues and, as always, the Indians' rights may be threatened. Yet with Indians in top positions in the Bureau of Indian Affairs, where they are much criticized by other Indians, with militant Indian movements such as Red Power and the American Indian Movement working for Indian rights, some progress may be possible. Naturally, there is a diversity of opinions among Indians, who disagree with each other, sometimes violently and destructively as at Wounded Knee in 1973, on what should be done. What happened there was as much Indian against Indian as Indians against whites. Even if the militancy of the 1960s and 1970s seems to have diminished, many of the changes it brought about may be regarded as permanent. But many problems remain, and the arguments, as always in Indian history, blend democracy with anarchy. But the Indians' wish to be regarded as Indians, peoples with a tragic, often awe-inspiring, sometimes glorious, always fascinating past, can no longer be challenged.

Below: Burying the Indian dead after Wounded Knee. Inset: The body of Big Foot after the massacre at Wounded Knee.

Opposite, inset top left: A Sioux family on a
reservation in the 1880s. Inset top right: Indians in
traditional dress at an Oregon round-up in 1977.
Main picture: An Arizona Indian woman making a
basket. Inset below: Iva Black Bear and three of
her children—modern Sioux.

This page, above: The skyscrapers that the
Mohawks helped to build. Right: A Yakima Indian
boy at the Ellensburg Rodeo, Washington.

INDEX

ACKNOWLEDGMENTS

The author and publisher would like to thank the following people who have helped in the preparation of this book: Thomas G Aylesworth, who edited it; Karin Knight, who prepared the index.

PICTURE CREDITS

All pictures were supplied by Peter Newark's Western Americana. In addition, the author would like to thank the following:

American Museum of Natural History: 58, 94-95 (bottom).
Courtauld Institute of Art, London: 36 (top).
David Lee Guss: 152.
Denver Public Library: 120 (left).
Kansas State Historical Society, Topeka: 13 (bottom right).
Library of Congress: 19 (top right), 48-49 (center), 74, 85 (center), 88 (bottom left), 125 (bottom).
Museum of the American Indian, New York City: 153.
National Archives: 68-69, 80 (top), 84 (left), 120 (center), 130 (top and bottom left), 134, 135 (top left), 136, 145.
Nebraska State Historical Society: 155 (left).
New York Historical Association: 37 (center left).
Oklahoma State Senate: 24 (bottom).
Oliver Yates Collection: 14 (top left), 23 (top center), 42-43, 114, 118, 126, 133 (left).
St. Joseph Museum, Missouri: 115.
Simon Trent: 35 (left).
Smithsonian Institution, National Anthropological Archives: 14 (bottom right and center), 34 (left), 36 (bottom), 41 (bottom), 50 (top), 54, 96 (bottom), 99 (top right), 100, 103 (right), 104 (bottom right), 107 (bottom center), 108 (top and bottom left), 110-111, 125 (top), 133 (right), 135 (top right), 132, 150 (top left), 151 (top and bottom left), 155 (right).
State Capitol, Helena, Montana: 45 (top left).
State Historical Society of Colorado: 78.
Trustees of the British Museum: 25 (center), 39 (right), 87 (top left).
Union Pacific Railroad Museum Collection: 71.
United States National Park Service: 14 (top center and bottom left), 46 (top), 46-47 (bottom), 49 (right), 50 (bottom).
Woolaroc Museum, Bartlesville, Oklahoma: 24 (top), 28-29, 47 (top left), 108 (top right), 148-149.